Bold, fresh, insightful and provocative. A
is perhaps Jon's best work yet.

—**Frank Viola**, author of G

Finally, a book for *all believers* about the beauty, worth, and high place of the church in the life of a saint. No denominational favoritism here. Instead, Jon and Graham move beyond centuries of division and factions to help God's people understand the lovely simplicity of what it means to be the church. From the very start, the authors' premises and passions are evident. Jon's inimitable style combines a likeably direct, no-nonsense approach to church life that offers much practical guidance to the subject. *58 to 0* is a *definitive must* for every Christian who is serious about sharing life in the Body of Christ.

—**Dr. Stephanie Bennett**, Florida, professor of Communication at Palm Beach Atlantic University, and author of *Communicating Love,* and two works of fiction, *Within the Walls* and *Breaking the Silence*

How did we go from 58 to 0? The answer to this question is quite profound, and not one you want to skip over. If these fifty-eight expressions of Jesus Christ were the norm, many would taste the very future heavenly age that Jesus talked about breaking into our present reality. Unfortunately, that is not the case. Do you know what these fifty-eight expressions are? If not, you'll want to find out. Let me caution you, however. Simply knowing what these fifty-eight expressions are will not change anything if the culprits that took us from fifty-eight to zero are not exposed. It is for this reason that I am honored to give my endorsement to Jon's latest work. It is a must read!

—**Jamal Jivanjee**, Tennessee, www.jamaljivanjee.com

There is a serious need for Christians today to understand their true identity as members of the priesthood who minister to one another as the N.T. affirms. This book couldn't be more necessary or timely for the Church today. A definite "must read" for every follower of Jesus.

—**Keith Giles**, California, author of *The Power of Weakness* and *"This Is My Body": Ekklesia as God Intended*

I read it once. That was powerful. I'll read it again and again.

—**Mitchell Bachman**, Iowa

In *58 to 0*, I see the heart and soul of Jon's writings since I first met him in 1979. I firmly believe that believers will see in this book the heart and soul of Christ.

As a historian, I agree with Jon that a radical shift took place in the Churches view of leadership and authority early in the 2nd Century. What was once the work of the Holy Spirit became the duty of a special class of leaders, separated in kind from the laity.

I grew up in Africa and had the privilege on several occasions of seeing 1st Century body life in the first believers in a community. I also witnessed the intrusion of the "organized" church, which replaced the "one-another" relationships that were occurring organically, with a structured authority. Jon, in *58 to 0*, has articulated the best description of what I saw in my childhood in Africa, and what I yearn to see in all of Christ's people.

I urge folks to put down what else they may be reading, and read this book. I have little doubt that an honest wrestling with the themes in the book will result in new paradigms, and a new appreciation for the person and work of Christ. I think this is the most important book that Jon has written.

—**Skeeter Wilson**, Washington, author of *Worthless People*
and the forthcoming *Crossing Rivers*

DEDICATION

I dedicate *58 to 0* to my dear friend and brother in Christ, Frank Viola. In God's mercy, since 1965 my journey has been centered on exalting Christ, but there were many "its" and "things" about Christ that clouded my path. The unique expression of Jesus through Frank accelerated my growth in the Son and unveiled more of the measureless treasures of Christ.

50 TO 0: HOW CHRIST LEADS THROUGH THE ONE ANOTHERS

Permission for wider usage of this material can be obtained through Ekklesia Press (address below) or go to: www.kingdomcitizenship.org

Publisher's Cataloging-in-Publication data

58 to 0 : how Christ leads through the one-anothers / Jon Zens ; Graham Wood, Editors.

   p. cm.

   ISBN 978-1-938480-05-8

1. Christian leadership. 2. Church. 3. Clergy --Office. 4. Pastoral theology. I. Fifty-eight to zero : how Christ leads through the one-anothers. II. Wood, Graham.

BV652.1 .Z46 2013
253 --dc23   2013951675

This volume is printed on acid free paper and meets ANSI Z39.48 standards.

Cover design and layout by: Rafael Polendo (polendo.net)

Printed in the United States of America

Ekklesia Press is a ministry to help authors get published and to publish works that are not deemed "profitable" by the mainstream publishing industry. Our goal is to put works into print that will impact and motivate followers of Christ to fulfill the Great Commission in an ever increasing way.

Ekklesia Press is an extension of www.kingdomcitizenship.org

Ekklesia Press
1401 South 64th Ave.
Omaha NE 68106

58 TO 0

HOW CHRIST LEADS
THROUGH THE ONE ANOTHERS

JON ZENS / GRAHAM WOOD, EDITORS

Ekklesia Press

Omaha, Nebraska

TABLE OF CONTENTS

FOREWORD

The fact that there is something like 58 one-anothers in the New Testament is a clear indication that we have definitely missed something in our modern day institutional concepts of leadership and ministry in the body of Christ. Many of those verses have to do with supporting and helping one another on a frequent (and even daily in some cases) basis. I believe that the basic problem in our understanding has to do with a lack of spiritual revelation concerning the Body of Christ.

Though the revelation of Christ's church being like a human body is exclusive to Paul, the flavor of it can be tasted throughout the whole New Testament. This is metaphoric imagery, plain and simple. Some people have told me that they find imagery to be a hindrance to understanding, and yet, it is used in the scriptures as the "key" to receiving the mysteries of the Kingdom of God. Jesus spoke in parables, which were symbolic stories, to make a spiritual point. But, He also referred to Himself metaphorically. He called Himself the Vine, the Bread, the Living Water, the Shepherd, the Ladder, the Door, the New Wine, the Word, the Light, the Bridegroom, the Lamb, Resurrection, the Way, the Truth, the Life, and the Temple. And these are just some of the images used in the gospel of John alone! The simple fact is that spiritual reality is best communicated through images and metaphors. But what do these metaphors mean? This is where revelation comes in. It's one thing to say that Jesus is the living water, it's quite another to spiritually understand that and experience Him as *your* water!

In like manner, Paul gives us (by the Holy Spirit) the metaphor of the Body. This revelation particularly implies the eternal purpose of God. In God's ageless purpose there is now a new Human, (Col. 3:10, 11) who is none other than Christ Himself. But now, this Christ has increased and has been incorporated into a new, many-membered Person. This Person is like no other! Of course, like any person, He is made up of a Head and a Body, (Eph. 1:22, 23). The Head and the Body together make up One New Human! Though the Head and the Body are distinct, they cannot be separate and are completely *one*. This is Paul's clear teaching in the letters to the Corinthians, the Colossians, and the Ephesians. Even though it is clear, it is not obvious! He calls this a mystery that needs to be revealed by the Spirit, (Eph.1:18-23).

Now that we have this as a quick foundation, perhaps we can gain some insight into such issues as leadership, ministry, the clergy-laity system, and such. All of these things must be taken into consideration within the context of *this* mystery. That is, within the context of the Body of Christ. And herein, I believe, lies the root problem for all the confusion and abuse within the so-called church today. *We are trying to have leadership, gifts and ministry outside of the context of proper body life.* For centuries we have been attempting to have the biblical experience and functioning of leadership and ministry and yet we have not even experienced true body life yet!

According to the New Testament, true "body-life" consists of a community of believers who are daily experiencing the life of the Head, and then sharing that life with one another and the world. All of the one-anothers found in the New Testament can be summed up within that one statement. All true leadership, gifts, and ministry come out from within the life of the Body. It can never happen the other way around... obviously!

Why don't we try a bold experiment? Why don't we all make an attempt at experiencing and living this kind of "body life" first? And then, let that body life teach us what it means to be leaders and ministers.

It's very difficult for us to understand what the scriptures teach about these matters unless we are living within the context to which it was written. Those letters were written to people who were living this kind of life! That's why those letters made sense and were applicable. In this book, *58 to 0*, Jon Zens does a stellar job of describing and explaining this kind of body life. He does it in light of the scriptures and of his own experiences. This book should definitely be a resource on the shelf of every believer out there that has an authentic vision and passion for God to recover His eternal purpose in and through His Church, which is His BODY.

—**Milt Rodriguez**, author of *New Day* and *The Community Life of God*

A WORD FROM GRAHAM WOOD

I found it both stimulating, yet disquieting to read and edit some of the articles now reappearing in this book, for it seems that some issues and problems which faced the early church require to be re-visited again and again in later generations.

A common thread is the issue of authority in the church, and as Norbert Ward simply states: 'There is one source of authority in the church. That authority is in the Lord Jesus Christ."

These writers understand that vital principle as they question many concepts and practices which challenge that authority, such as the stultifying church institutionalism, the dominance of the clergy, the entrenched 'clergy/laity' division, and not least, the role of the omni-competent "one pastor" rule, among others.

As J. Lawrence Burkholder reminds us, churches need to recover their role as discerning communities, by challenging the many human traditions within the status quo, and re-visiting what Jesus has really said about *ekklesia*.

The message from these writers needs to be heard loud and clear by all sectors of the visible church, for to be "reformed" and "renewed" as churches is not a static situation, but one of constant movement toward the goal of the ideal, the will of God in Christ Jesus.

John Howard Yoder summarizes something of the challenge we face:

> The conclusion is inescapable that the multiplicity of ministries is not a mere happenstance of only superficial significance, but a specific work of grace and a standard for the church.

Perhaps the modern church is being challenged by Elijah's confrontation with Israel: "how long will you halt between two opinions?" Will we tamely submit to and serve monolithic church structures and practices, driven by tradition only, or will we follow Christ through the simple church pattern he has revealed for his church?

—**Graham Wood**, York, UK

PART ONE: JON ZENS

"YOU ARE ALL BROTHERS AND SISTERS"

CHAPTER 1

SETTING THE STAGE

A few years ago I was having coffee with my friend Gordon Gillesby, and he said, "You know, Jon, when you boil things down, all of your books are challenging aspects of the problem of control and the misunderstanding of 'authority.' I think you need to write a book dealing with these matters." *58 to 0: How Christ Leads Through the One Anothers* has emerged as a result of that conversation, and years of observing how churches function.

The truth is, the starting point for the religious paradigm we've inherited is "leadership." Over the years I've seen places where the pastor leaves and the body steps up to the plate in the interim. Often, people will enjoy the body ministry, but usually after about 4-6 months people start clamoring for a pastor. The office of pastor has been created by tradition. There is no New Testament (N.T.) basis for it. Thus for a church to "fill the position" of pastor is a huge step in the wrong direction in the first place.

I think in Western churches there is a lopsided emphasis on "leaders." For example, in a blurb about the Global Leadership Summit hosted at the Willow Creek Community Church in Illinois it was said, "Thousands of leaders across North America gather together to hear speakers from all over the world, participate in interactive dialogue, and have practical training—which focuses on helping the church raise up leaders, as well as helping leaders in churches develop their leadership gifts."

"Leadership...leadership... leadership." It is interesting to compare the number of books on leadership and conferences for leaders versus books and conferences on cultivating body-life among the priesthood of all believers! The deck is stacked! One would think that leadership must be the largest topic in the NT!

The key point is this: in the NT, the organic way for everything to develop is through the functioning of all the living stones together. The starting point of assembly-life is the priesthood of all believers as a living reality. To focus on, or be concerned about "leadership" without a lovingly functioning body is just a disaster hiding in the bushes. My counsel to new groups is to function together with leadership as a non-issue for two to five years.

Assembly-life is the context for decision-making. Leaders are never mentioned in what Jesus teaches about problem-resolution in Matthew 18:15-20. The final context is "take it to the congregation." The N.T. letters were written to assemblies, not to leaders. The Corinthian church had a lot of issues, but Paul assumed that the body could take care of them—"when you come together as a body," (1 Cor. 5:4). Leaders are never chided for failing in their responsibilities.

Traditional church practice puts decision-making, and the nuts-and-bolts of church machinery in the hands of "leaders." The N.T. puts the responsibility of carrying out the will of Christ on the shoulders of the entire body. In the lopsidedness of our leader-dependence, we have lost the vision of an assembly listening to the voice of Christ together. To focus on leaders without having first a functioning body is to put the proverbial cart before the horse—with far-reaching dire consequences.

Most groups in America are not ready for "leadership." The attention given to leadership is usually very premature. Most agree that specific giftedness is revealed only after the *ekklesia* takes hold. But at the same time many feel that the reason many groups outside the institutional church fall apart is because they lack good leadership. Why does everything always seem to come back to some aspect of leadership in Western churches—and in groups worldwide where our style has been exported?

The real issue comes down to this—is the life of Christ coming to expression through all the persons in the group? Is that Life sufficient to guide, enrich and grow all the parts as they lift up Christ together? I must put it like this: if a group is filled with Jesus and his guidance, "leaders" will probably not be on their minds; if a group lacks the fullness of Jesus, they will probably become fixated on the need for "leaders."

Interestingly, in my experience, in almost every case where a group outside the institutional church formally recognized elders, the expression of Christ by the whole body went downhill quickly.

I have increasingly come to the conviction that if assemblies had outside help from those who lay the foundation of Christ among God's people, there would be less concern about "leaders," and then proper focus could be given to Jesus' presence among the brothers and sisters.

The Bride of Christ is a family. Families have moms and dads who help the younger ones. If we end up spending an inordinate amount of time worrying about how the older ones are recognized, function and relate to one another, we will miss the beauty of Jesus in the midst of his flock. Compared to the information on body-life in the NT, the space we give to leadership issues is way out of proportion, and is filled with mistaken assumptions.

I'm not interested in throwing out the baby, the bathwater, or the tub—as they are given reality by Christ. Let me give a true illustration. At several conferences I've heard speakers go into great detail about how our goal should be a city-church with many house-churches networking together, and with apostles-prophets floating around in ministry. Much they say is commendable, but the problem is that the audience, and the church-at-large, is a zillion miles from any of this ever being a reality. Most people I know are struggling to find a few other people to come along on the journey! And that's my point about groups being overly concerned about "leaders"—they are miles and miles from being ready to even give a moment to such issues.

Consider Hebrews 12:15. The verb *episcopeo* is used there, but is totally lost in most English translations. The author is saying, "take the oversight" of one another. Here is a "leadership" verb, used elsewhere of "overseers" (elders), but is here being applied as a responsibility for the whole body. So, again, if a group of Christians cannot from their inception grow in their functioning as a priesthood of *mutual overseers*, how can we ever expect some future overseers to arise as servants to the body? Everything must flow and arise out of Life; in the traditional practice of church everything pretty much hinges on leadership—often brought in from the outside. If the life of Christ is throbbing in and coming to expression through each believer in community, leadership will be a non-issue—an "it" that is usually very distracting.

Some would say, "The elders or leaders within that local church gathering must be acknowledged and identified in order to preserve and defend the pure doctrine of our faith." I think this statement shows that we need to see more deeply the Holy Spirit resources in the body. It is true that the mature persons in the *ekklesia* can be of critical help in the mutual care of each other. But the N.T. first and foremost teaches that *the whole body* is to be involved, not primarily the elders. For example, the exhortation to "test the spirits" is given to all the brothers and sisters, not just to "leaders." Why? Because they all possess the "anointing." Paul's directive about restorative care in Galatians 6:1-2 is given to all the saints. All of Paul's corrections to the multiple issues in the Corinthian *ekklesia* were set in front of the body. Leaders are not mentioned. In Matthew 18, the final context rests in "tell it to the *ekklesia*." Again, nothing was said about leaders. I do not think we have begun to grasp the significance of the fact that the N.T. letters were written to *ekklesias*, not leaders. As I pointed out above, the writer of Hebrews told all of the Lord's people to "oversee one another," using a "leadership" verb from which we get our English word, "Episcopal."

We would do well, I think, to focus on knowing Christ and sharing Him with one another. If the rivers of Christ's living water were flowing from the saints, as they should, is it not possible that "leadership" would recede into the shadows? I hope that you would agree that if we pursued Christ's leadership, presence and expression in a Spirit-led way, all this other "stuff" would be put in its place. If Christ is not the functional Leader of most churches, what right do we have to fill books about the alleged need for "church leaders"?

CHAPTER 2

LIFE ON THE BOTTOM RUNG: THE KING WHO WASHED FEET

Around 1870, John Christoph Blumhardt observed, "In every age, whatever is difficult is understood only by a few. That to which everyone runs; that which everyone, as part of the herd, simply accepts—that is easy. So, not where the many dash and run, but where only a few are to be seen—there lies the deeper truth. And so today Jesus' 'little flock' consists of those who are not content with run-of-the-mill Christianity, but who trust in the one who is greater, having hope in a high goal for humankind," (*Thy Kingdom Come: A Blumhardt Reader*, Vernard Eller, ed., Eerdmans, 1980, p. 81).

History reveals that many rushed after the easy way of fleshly control and power in the post-apostolic church, and only a few have ever pursued the difficult road of servanthood that Jesus displayed. In this chapter we will look at the clear direction Jesus gave during His earthly life.

Though a King, He lived His life on the bottom rung of the ladder. From this position, He was low to the ground, near the feet that He would wash.

As most of you know, over the past fifty years there have been hundreds of books written for church leaders, and those aspiring to be leaders. One of them is called *Jesus, CEO*. Such a title epitomizes the attempts to cast Jesus in the world's business model.

What frustrates me is that such books begin with the status quo, assume it is correct, and then suggest ways to tweak it and make it better. Such books take some of what Jesus said and try to apply it to the way "church" is usually done. An example of this is Tony Jones' *The Church Is Flat*. This book presents a number of superb thoughts about re-thinking church, but it doesn't cut to the quick regarding the sacred cow of "the pastor." The narrative just assumes that "clergy" will be part of what is necessary.

The problem is that what Jesus taught cannot be made to "fit" into status quo church. The exact things that Jesus pointedly expressed are squeezed through grids that result in a customized and controlled Christ. These books relate many good things, but when it comes to that critical moment of taking Him seriously, His words cannot have full sway, because if they did, the house of cards would come tumbling down.

It needs to be appreciated, then, that there is a leader-centric paradigm lurking under almost every religious stone. The way of Jesus stands diametrically opposed to this paradigm.

What did Jesus impart to His apostles and disciples concerning how they should function in His kingdom? Whatever it was, it was radical. It went against the leader-dominant ways of both Judaism and paganism. Remember, He is saying these things to those who will be people of great influence in His realm.

LUKE 22:24-27

[24]And there was also rivalry among them concerning which of them should be looked upon as the greatest. [25]Jesus said to them, "The kings of the Gentiles lord it over them; and those who exercise authority over them call themselves Benefactors. [26]But you are not to be like that. Instead, the greatest among you should be like the youngest, and the one who rules like the one who serves. [27]For who is greater, the one who is at the table or the one who serves? Is it not the one who is at the table? But I am among you as one who serves.

The Lord gave His answer to this in-house competitive strife about who would be on the top rung of the ladder. In responding, He discards a nearby cultural model, and sets forth His mind-blowing way of life. Jesus flat out rejects the Gentile worldly model in which the subjects are lorded over and put in a dependent status where they must call their leaders "Benefactors." This is a typical top-down way of governing, consisting of those in power and those in subjection. All of human history is pretty well summed up by this way of doing things. Jesus categorically tells His people, "You are not to be this way."

The road to greatness that Jesus unfolded was a new paradigm, and was certainly shocking to the disciples' ears. "If you want to be great, you will live at the bottom of the ladder, serving those sitting at the table."

"The greatest will be like the youngest." The youngest in a group has zero status. They are the new kid on the block. They are at the bottom of the pecking order. They lack experience, and have not earned any clout or "say" in the group. Jesus turns the tables by suggesting that *those who will have the greatest influence will function as those with no authority or status.*

To comprehend how off-the-charts Christ's remarks were, we must be reminded of how status-conscious life was in the 1st Century. From waking in the morning to going to bed at night, people were looking at their daily contacts in terms of where they were at in the social hierarchy of the day. Needless to say, the great bulk of folks were at various notches at the bottom of the social ladder. "Simply put, most people in the Greco-Roman world were constantly conscious that their social status was potentially in flux, moving up or down by accumulating honor or shame, respectively" (Jeff Miller, "What A Shame!" CBE Arise, July, 2013). Thus, for Christ to suggest that the "place of honor" was to be a slave doing the bidding of others was way outside the box in that time, and remains so even today.

But Jesus was no ivory tower philosopher. He pointed to Himself to show His followers how He lived day-by-day: *"I am among you as one who serves."* Christ lived out life not at the top, but at the very bottom. This also helps us understand why He was chastised by the Jewish leaders for befriending the riffraff, lowest-class "sinners."

MARK 9:33-37

[33]They came to Capernaum. When he was in the house, he asked them, "What were you arguing about on the road?" [34]But they kept quiet because on the way they had argued about who was the greatest. [35]Sitting down, Jesus called the Twelve and said, "Anyone who wants to be first must be the very last, and the servant of all." [36]He took a little child whom he placed among them. Taking the child in his arms, he said to them, [37]"Whoever welcomes one of these little children in my name welcomes me; and whoever welcomes me does not welcome me but the one who sent me."

Again, their arguing about greatness is the backdrop for Jesus' teaching. They might have said, "Now just wait a minute, Jesus, are you saying that in order for a person to be first [Greek, *protos*], they have to be last [Greek, *eschatos*] and a table-waiter [Greek, *diakonos*, deacon] to boot? That doesn't make any sense. How can one be at the top of the ladder by being a slave (about the least esteemed position in our culture) on the bottom rung of the ladder?" And Jesus replied, "I have brought the heavenly realm of my kingdom to earth. In my realm the bottom is the top. The one who puts himself on the top will ultimately be brought down low. My kingdom is not of this world. Am I being served at a table, or am I bringing food to those sitting at the table? Go figure."

Why did Jesus use a child to make a point? It was because in Christ's day, children were low on the social ladder. "Children," Bruce Malina notes, "had little status within the community or family. A minor child was on par with a slave.... The orphan was the stereotype of the weakest and most vulnerable member of society," (*Social-Science Commentary on the Synoptic Gospels,* Fortress Press, 1992, p. 238). Yet Jesus made it clear that to receive a child was to receive Him. Again, Jesus identified with the lowest persons in His surroundings.

MATTHEW 20:25-28

[25]Jesus called them together and said, "You know that the rulers of the Gentiles lord it over them, and their high officials exercise authority over them. [26]Not so with you. Instead, whoever wants to become great among you must be your servant, [27]and whoever wants to be first must be your slave— [28]just as the Son of Man did not come to be served, but to serve, and to give his life as a ransom for many."

This Gentile way of rulers exercising authority over their subjects was to have no place in Christ's kingdom. It was to be cast out like a demon. "Not like this among you." Exercising authority over people is simply out of the question in Christ's kingdom.

Once again, the grand example of bottom-rung living was Christ. He was not sent to the earth to be served, but rather to serve others by laying down His life on their behalf. The person being served at the table had the status. The one serving by bringing out the grub had no status.

MATTHEW 23:8-12

[8]"But you are not to be called 'Rabbi,' for you have one Teacher, and you are all brothers/sisters. [9]And do not call anyone on earth 'father,' for you have one Father, and he is in heaven. [10]Nor are you to be called Leaders, for you have one Leader, the Messiah. [11]The greatest among you will be your servant. [12]For those who exalt themselves will be humbled, and those who humble themselves will be exalted.

Bruce Davidson and Darryl Erkel have articles on religious titles in Part 2, chapters 3 and 4, so my comments here will be brief. Jesus is in the midst of some rather straightforward words to the Pharisees. I would like to note a few central thoughts based on this portion of Matthew.

Language reflects peoples' practice. Religious titles give indication that people are divided into upper and lower echelons, like "clergy" and "laity." Titles that divide people into classes have no place in the Lord's vineyard. Granting a few titles is a flat-out denial of the reality of a Body of brothers and sisters. This is a serious problem on the horizontal level.

Religious titles also create issues on the vertical level. *To call someone "teacher" deflects us from following Jesus as our sole Teacher. To call someone "father," as the Roman Catholics do, diverts us from our only Father in heaven.* But here's the big one—calling someone a "leader" turns us aside from looking to our one Leader, the Messiah.

Since 150AD, it became commonplace for a few to be titled "leaders" — "the bishop will take care of that matter" or "the pastor has been sick the past few days." Given the overwhelming emphasis and dependence on "leaders" in Christianity, is it any marvel that Jesus is not the functional Teacher and Leader in what calls itself "church"?

MARK 10:35-40

The disciples on multiple occasions argued over who would be the greatest in His kingdom. Jesus asks, "Do you love me?" We ask, "Can we sit at your right hand and your left hand in your Kingdom?" (H. Nouwen, *In the Name of Jesus*, p. 77). The disciples wanted the glory of positions connected to power, but they did not know yet that the road to greatness is paved with suffering.

In response to the inquiry concerning front row seats in the kingdom, Jesus says, "You have no clue what you are asking for. Are you ready for a deep cup of affliction and a baptism of anguish?"

The church went through cycles of persecution, some brutal, until the advent of Constantine in 307AD. "[Before Constantine, often] simply being a Christian was a crime against the state. In 313AD, as a result of an edict from the Emperor of Rome, the position changed completely.... The Christian Church had now become an accepted institution of the Empire," (O'Grady, pp. 73, 74).

Once the visible church was sanctioned by the State, life on the bottom rung was discarded, and it became entangled in worldly *power plays* and politics. Further, the way of suffering was traded in for protection by Emperors.

JOHN 13 – THE KING WASHES FEET

While all of Scripture is a wonderful revelation of Christ, it cannot be wrong to view chapters 13-17 of John as special and important. Jesus is on the eve of His death, and His words and actions in these chapters show, in a unique way, what was on His heart as the New Exodus drew near.

Jesus knew that Father had put everything under His feet. He was truly a King. He could have demanded all people to worship Him, but instead He took a towel, assumed the lowliest of positions, and washed the disciples' feet.

Of all things He could have said or done, He knew that the posture of washing feet was the most critical visual to give His people at the end of His earthly life. "If I, your Lord and Teacher, have washed your feet, then you also should wash one another's feet. I have given you an example, that out of my love and life you should do as I have done for you."

Their understanding that day was probably not real deep. Jesus let them know that "you do not realize now what I am doing, but later you will understand." When the Spirit came on the Day of Pentecost onwards, their minds and hearts would be opened up to the significance of Jesus' words and deeds. "At first His disciples did not understand all this. Only after Jesus was glorified in resurrection did they realize that these things had been written of Him, and that they had done these things to Him," (John 12:16).

To cap off His earthly life, King Jesus once again underscores that His Life is about being last in order to be first, about washing feet, not being in charge of people—about life on the bottom rung.

There are certainly some matters in the N.T. that we might wish were clearer. But, the Gospel passages we have surveyed leave no doubt that Jesus intended to build an *ekklesia* in which there was no hierarchy, no exercising authority over others, no separation of His people into Titled and Non-titled, and no greatness without suffering on the bottom rung.

Did the future visible church, after 150AD, remember and practice Jesus' ways? *Absolutely not!* Ray C. Stedman uttered these most profound, but tragic, words:

"Throughout twenty centuries the church has virtually ignored these words" (http://www.ldolphin.org/pastorauth.html).

In Chapter 4 we will uncover and explore what went wrong. But in Chapter 3 we want to see how the *ekklesia* carries on the life and ministry of Jesus Christ as His Bride and Body.

Chapter 2 is an edited and expanded version of a talk Jon gave at the 6th Searching Together Gathering, July, 2005, entitled, "Those with the Most Influence Live Like Those with No Authority."

CHAPTER 3

A KINGDOM OF TABLE-WAITERS: JESUS' LIFE CONTINUES IN THE EKKLESIA

Picture the Bride of Christ sitting around a humongous table at the wedding feast of the Lamb. They are all waiting for the banquet to be served. The kitchen door swings open and out comes Jesus, bringing His Beloved a lavish meal. "He will dress Himself to serve, will have them recline at the table, and will come and wait on them," (Luke 12:37).

JOHN 13, BEING THE EXAMPLE:

Every moment of His time on earth was spent listening to Father and serving others. As His hour drew near, Jesus attended to His disciples by washing their feet. The final visual He gave them before death was that of a slave caring for dusty feet. Then, when history is finished, in the New Heaven/New Earth, we find Christ table-waiting for His people who come from the four corners of the earth.

What was to happen during the interim between His returning to His Father, and His glorious return? *He is to continue His divine Life on earth through His Body of many parts as diakonoi* (deacons), that is, as table-waiters.

JOHN 14-17, HE IS IN US:

As Jesus' earthly life winds down, He tells them that He must return to His Father. He has to say "good-bye" for a while. But He promises them that they will not be left as orphans. Father and Son will send the Helper—the Holy Spirit—to them.

Jesus announced to them, "I will come to you!" This promise was fulfilled on the Day of Pentecost when Christ came to the *ekklesia* in the Holy Spirit. Because of the historic emphasis on the final, glorious coming of Christ, the Day of Pentecost is generally not thought of as a coming of Christ.

His coming on that day was a pivotal reality showing that the Life of Messiah would continue on earth through the Body of Christ. Jesus pointed out, it is "the Father living in Me who is doing His work; I am in the Father and the Father in

Me." Likewise, with the coming of Christ in the Spirit, He stated to His people, "you are in Me and I am in you." Jesus lived by Father's life dwelling in Him; so now we live by Christ's life dwelling in us. Christ was Father on earth; the *ekklesia* is Christ on earth.

JESUS IS IN THE BODY

If it is asked, "Where is Christ on earth after He ascended to Father's right hand?" the only proper answer is—*in the ekklesia where His life flows out of those who believe.* The ekklesia is the Body of Christ on earth. "Christ's Body" is not a metaphor, but a *reality*.

I was always taught that the "Body of Christ" was just a picture. But the N.T. will not sustain that notion. For example, in Acts 9 Paul was traveling with authorization to make prisoners of believers, both men and women. As he neared Damascus, the first words of Jesus to Paul were, "Saul, Saul, why *Me* are you persecuting?" Paul asked Him who He was, and His reply is astounding—*"I am Jesus whom you are persecuting."* Why can the Lord utter such a remark? Because *Christ is in each believer,* and when you mess with His Body, you are messing with Him!

This helps us to understand why Jesus said, "if anyone causes one of these little ones who believe in Me to sin, it would be better for them to be thrown into the sea with a large millstone tied around their neck." If you are hurting believers, you are hurting Christ.

Another example is found in 1 Corinthians 1. These people were clustering around personalities—"Paul's my favorite," "Peter's my man," "Apollos is awesome." What is one aspect of Paul's response to this sin? *"Is Christ divided?"* Humans were gathering around gifted persons, but Paul saw in this action Christ being sliced into pieces like a pie. As Frank Viola put it, "Dividing a body of believers is like taking a butcher knife to Jesus Christ and cutting Him up into pieces. It's very serious. Paul gives us this image in 1 Corinthians 1" (http://frankviola.org/2013/03/13/rethinkingspiritualgifts5/).

Jesus said, "I will remain in the world no more, but they are still in the world, and I am coming to You." We must have a revelation of this reality—*just as Father was in the world through Christ's incarnation, so after He returned to Father, He is now in the world through His Body,* the *ekklesia.*

EPHESIANS 3:10, GOD'S INTENTION

Why, then, are we left on earth? Paul told us in Ephesians 3:10—"it was God's intention that now, through the *ekklesia*, the manifold wisdom of God should be made known to the rulers and authorities in the heavenly realms, according to His eternal purpose which He accomplished in Christ Jesus our Lord." In a word, the *ekklesia*—because His life is in them—displays and expresses the riches and treasures of Christ, both to one another and to the culture in which they live.

For the purposes of this book, one of the key ways the *ekklesia* displays the Life of Christ on earth is by embodying His Body dynamic—"you are all brothers and sisters" —and rejecting the top-down model of rule—"not so among you." This has always been a struggle for believers, and as we will see in Chapter 4, the visible church early on in post-apostolic history adopted top-down authoritarianism to the hilt.

How does Christ's life in this regard come to expression in cultures all over the world? How can the *ekklesia* be counter-cultural in pursuing His kingdom, without destroying valid, or neutral, aspects of any culture? Wolfgang Simson suggests:

> If, for example, the church is incarnated in a highly militaristic and urban culture, where powerful kings have ruled society for a long time and the ordinary folk, deeply insecure, still feel the need to be in the shadow of a strong general and leader...what would a church in this culture look like? The church would have an aroma of an army, organized according to military rank and file, where everyone has a title or a badge to show their position, and where the all-important role of a senior leader is beyond question, (*Houses that Change the World*, OM Publishing, 2001, p. 236).

I certainly do not claim to have all the answers for such cultural challenges, but at a minimum it would seem that such an approach in a strongly hierarchical social setting seriously compromises the way of Christ. "Not so among you" implies a radical, counter-cultural way of community. Patience, longsuffering and wisdom are certainly necessary in such cases, but to let rank, titles and senior leaders dominate from the outset will snuff out the light of Christ's expression.

JESUS WAITED ON TABLES, NOW HIS BODY DOES

Without doubt, the most fundamental and pervasive words used in the N.T. to describe believers were connected in the 1st Century to the very bottom of the social ladder. These words depicted people who took care of the needs and did the bidding of others, like waiting on those reclined at a table. Of course, these same words were used of Jesus. Words like *serve, servant,* and *slave* are used hundreds of times to portray the posture and function of believers— "serve one another in love," "you serve the Lord Christ."

However, something very tragic happened in some Bible versions. The way the word "servant" was often translated conjured up images of professionalism and status, instead of table waiting. The King James Version many times rendered "servant" as "minister," as in 1 Timothy 1:12, "putting me into the ministry," or 1 Corinthians 3:5, "ministers by whom you believed." Historically, the word "minister" has been linked to those who are called "clergy." Interestingly, when the word is used of sister Phoebe in Romans 16:1, then suddenly they translated it as "servant"!

"WHEN YOU COME TOGETHER"

Christ continues His life on earth through His Body, the *ekklesia*. Following His steps, the brothers and sisters are a realm of table-waiters. This is a kingdom where no one is on the top rung—except Jesus. In fact, in the *ekklesia* there are no rungs because Jesus said, "You are all brothers and sisters."

How, then, do believers function when they come together as the *ekklesia*? I deal with more details in a section of *The Pastor Has No Clothes*, pp. 48-59, but here I would like to share some broad strokes that get to the heart of the question.

1. Traditionally, when believers gather together, the focus has been on leaders who occupy offices and who are "over" the church. The truth is that the *ekklesia* is never without leadership—*Christ is the Leader.* In fact, Jesus was most explicit when He said to His followers, "Neither be called 'leaders,' because your Leader is One, the Christ." If we are leader-centric, the odds are high we have already abandoned His loving oversight.

2. We all tend to be like Israel—we want a king, some human "in control." The top-down, worldly approach to church is reflected in these words, typical of the leader-centered system:

   > An orderly church needs one overseer, one shepherd, and one pastor. The pastor needs to have general oversight of the education, music, youth, activities and any other ministries in a flock.... Allow this old veteran to observe that chaos easily develops where no one is in charge. If the church is to be one flock, it needs one shepherd, (Frank Owen, 1981).

Such sentiments betray the facts that the *ekklesia* does have one Shepherd, Jesus, that Someone is in charge, Jesus, and that as most everyone has seen, chaos develops even when churches have "the pastor"!

It takes a revelation from above to wean us away from resting in human leadership, and functionally trusting Christ to guide His flock.

1. Thus, when believers come together, they freely confess that they want Jesus to guide the gathering by the Holy Spirit. Whether in spontaneity or with planning, they want all expressions of Christ to be Spirit-led.

2. This is an extremely vulnerable way to function. Without church bulletins or other props, it can be scary to ask Christ by the Spirit to flow with His life through the brothers and sisters. Notice in the open meeting described in 1 Corinthians 14 that no persons or person is "leading" up front. Yes, they had some issues, but Paul does not squelch the open participation—"each of you has a song, a teaching, a revelation."

What will occur in the typical Sunday church service is already known. As Clyde Reid observed in 1966, "Basically, we do not want anything to happen on Sunday morning that will upset our daily routine. So, subconsciously we structure the service in order to assure safe, predicable, comfortable results," *(The God Evaders).*

The Holy Spirit is like wind. You cannot put Her in a box, and you cannot know ahead of time, which way She will blow.

1. When the brothers and sisters are present together, "leadership" does happen. A group may not have "leaders," but that does not mean they are not "being led." The issue is: *Is Christ leading by the Spirit, or are humans leading in the flesh?*

2. Jesus' leadership of the *ekklesia* will be fluid, floating, and shared—varying each time they come together, as the Lord leads. We might call this phenomenon "leadership in the moment." We are used to looking to the same person(s) to guide believers' gatherings. Instead, we should be looking to Christ to lead the sisters and brothers in their expressions of Him.

3. Christ's view of "leadership" is upside down from the way the world functions. It is from the bottom of the ladder, not the top. The truth is, in Christ's kingdom *there is to be no ladder!* How can a bunch of table-waiters have a ladder? They are all at the bottom serving Him and one another.

4. "Leadership" from Jesus occurs in people through example, maturity, humility, and brokenness, not positions, titles, intimidation, guilt and fear.

WHAT ABOUT HEBREWS 13:17?

"Obey your leaders and submit to their authority..." (NIV)

This verse has been used to badger the saints concerning their need to "submit" to leaders. But given the author's purpose in writing Hebrews, such a use of 13:17 is totally out of context.

The NIV translation of Hebrews 13:17 perpetuates some serious misunderstandings. The Greek verb *peitho* means to persuade, and it is in the middle voice— "let yourselves be persuaded by those..." The contextual reason why the author is exhorting the people to be persuaded is because the guides were good examples of holding onto Christ in the New Covenant.

There is no basis for the phrase "their authority." As Leon Morris notes, "there is nothing in the Greek to correspond to the NIV's 'their authority'; *hypeikete* means simply 'yield' or 'submit'" (*The Expositor's Bible Commentary,* Vol. 12, p. 152). To "let yourself be persuaded" implies discernment, not a blind following of people just because they occupy an alleged "office." These people needed to let themselves be persuaded by these particular guides because they were excellent examples of people who were focusing on Christ, and not going back under the beggarly elements of the Law.

HEBREWS 12:15, MUTUAL OVERSIGHT

While church leaders will milk Hebrews 13:17 for all it is worth, you never hear them talk about the implications of Hebrews 12:15.

Interestingly, in Hebrews 12:15—"see to it that no one comes short of the grace of God"— the verb used there is *episcopeo*, "to oversee." We get our English word "Episcopal" from this root. The noun "overseer" comes from this verb. But in Hebrews 12:15 *the whole body of believers* is to participate in the "oversight" of one another. Compared to the 58 "one-anothers" in the New Testament, the inordinate emphasis on "leadership" that is found in the Western church is absent. In a family, the focus is not on those at the top—the focus is on relationships. In an institution, you must focus on leadership in order to get things done. As Mary Pipher perceptively notes, "Too often [health] institutions are about the needs of the institution, not of the patients" (*Another Country,* 2000, p. 167).

In light of these verses from Hebrews, here are some further thoughts:

1. *Episcopeo* ("oversee") is viewed as a "leadership" word, yet in Hebrews 12:15 it is applied to the *whole body.* Everyone, in various ways, participates in Body oversight.

2. The general problem, it seems to me, is that other things get in the way of all the one-anothering perspectives emphasized in the New Testament. One huge distraction is that groups become concerned about "the need for leadership." Shouldn't the life of Christ be flowing in deepening relationships in which the *caring oversight* of one another is displayed *long before* there is any thought given to oversight that might be recognized by the Body?

3. Most people are unaware of the huge chasm between the recognition of "elders" in the New Testament, and our practice of leadership. They read about "elders," conclude that "elders" are necessary, and that steps should be taken to set them apart. Some believe that you are not really a church unless you have "elders."

The reality is that long-term *relationships and functions* precede any recognition by the *ekklesia.* Paul said, "Know those who labor among you." The N.T. envisions gifts being discerned as time goes on among believers who are sharing Christ's life together. The unbiblical practice of the Western church is to give people titles and positions that *are not rooted in long-term relationships.*

MATTHEW 25:31-40, "YOU DID IT TO ME"

At the end of history when all the dead are raised, Christ's kingdom of table-waiters will be recognized. Again, this passage highlights the intimate union between Jesus and believers. He tells them that what they did for others was in fact done to *Him.*

He reminds the sheep about the times that they provided food and drink, showed hospitality, gave clothing, and visited the sick. All these actions were done by people with no status, no ladder to climb. Notice that the righteous do not say, "Lord, we wondered when you would recognize the many things we've done for You." No, they say, "When did we do that?" They had no interest in keeping track of their "good deeds." The Lord has to inform them of what they did to Him.

Jesus on earth was among His people as *one who served.* His Bride on earth is a realm of table-waiters, *serving others.* In the age to come, Christ will again be *serving* an eternal banquet of Himself to the *ekklesia* He purchased with His own blood.

"If I then washed your feet, you ought to wash one another's feet." It doesn't get any better than that! A kingdom where we are all brothers and sisters, a kingdom that says "no" to hierarchy, a kingdom where no titles are needed, and a kingdom with no "leaders," for their Leader is One, the Messiah.

For Further Reflection:

Gordon D. Fee, "Praying and Prophesying in the Assemblies: 1 Corinthians 11:2-16," *Discovering Biblical Equality,* Ronald W. Pierce, and Rebecca Merrill Groothuis, general editors; Gordon D. Fee, contributing editor, IVP, 2004, pp. 142-160

Frank Viola, "A New Species," *From Eternity to Here,* David C. Cook, 2009, pp. 223-289

"The waning of the Enthusiasm was no uniform process, nor one that can be definitely dated or documented. But there is one thing we can say. By about the year A.D. 65 the three great apostolic leaders, Peter, Paul, and James, were dead; and from that time till the end of the century is one of the darkest periods of Christian history . . . . To pass from the year 65 to the year 100 has been compared to passing through a tunnel; but, we might add, it is the kind of tunnel that pierces a frontier range of mountains; when we emerge from it we find ourselves in another climate; the air is cooler and the landscape more ordinary . . . . We have passed from the region of creative Enthusiasm into a region of growing ecclesiastical system and order."

— **Alexander B. Macdonald**, *Christian Worship in the Primitive Church*, T & T Clark, 1934, p. 69

CHAPTER 4

WHAT WENT WRONG? LIVING ORGANISM TO LIFELESS INSTITUTION

Christ imparted to His followers, by word and deed, that in His kingdom there would be no hierarchy, neither power plays nor titles. Instead, we are among sisters and brothers where sacrificial love and mutual foot washing prevail.

Jesus demonstrated that He is building His *ekklesia* on earth. Christ told the disciples that when His resurrected body went back to the Father, He would continue His body life all over the earth. His reign increases in His kingdom in which all are brothers and sisters, and no one is "over" others.

But the annals of history reveal something went wrong, *dreadfully wrong!* Before we get into some of the details, here's a snapshot of a few key moments that give us insight as to how and when the way of Jesus was flagrantly cast aside.

1. Around 150AD Clement made a distinction between "priest" and "laity." This set in motion the unbiblical divide of "clergy" and "laity," the "ordained" and the non-ordained parishioners. Those "ordained" are "officially" invested with the priestly functions by titled offices. This was a new, human-based type of church order and authority.

2. Around 250AD the practice of "one-bishop rule" took root, and each bishop's rule was defined territorially, (see Judy Schindler, Part 2, Chapter 9).

3. Around 325AD the Emperor Constantine created a new religion mixed with paganism, called it "Christianity," and made it the official religion of the Roman Empire. From this point on, the civil rulers would have a heavy presence in what occurred in the visible church.

Thus, what was birthed as Christ our life, the Spirit-led wind of the *ekklesias*, morphed into a power-based, hierarchy-fed institution.

The expression of Christ through the Spirit functioned in a beautiful way in the early church. There was no "institution" in the beginning. The "institution" started taking shape from 150AD onwards. As this institutional system unfolded, the Spirit of Christ became unnecessary, for the "institution" saw itself as the dispenser of grace. This is not to say there was no Spirit life anywhere, but it is to say that as the "institution" became more and more powerful, the Holy Spirit became less and less a part of the mix.

THE STRIKING FEATURES OF THE 1ST CENTURY EKKLESIA

In 1st Century pagan religions and Judaism all had these basic characteristics:

1. Specific experts who led the religious practices

2. Specific places (temples) where the people came to practice the religion

3. Specific religious rituals that were carried out in designated ways and times

It is precisely these three marks that *were utterly absent from the early church.* They functioned with no "clergy" (all of the saints were "clergy," the Lord's "inheritance"), no religious buildings (they met "home to home"), and no set rituals ("each one of you has a song, a teaching, etc.").

However, as was mentioned above, this simplicity was compromised in the 2nd and 3rd Centuries with the introduction of the leader/common people distinction, and the increasing focus on the "bishop" as the one to whom submission must be given.

The third major capitulation occurred in the 4th Century when the new form of church was recognized as the central religion of the Roman Empire by Constantine, and granted special privileges by the State.

From that time on, the relation of the Christian Church to secular rulers, as well as the growth of the Church's own secular power, was bound to influence the development of the Christian religion itself, (O'Grady, p. 73).

CONSTANTINE: THE FUSION OF CHURCH AND STATE

Obviously, Constantine was an opportunistic person. From 306 – 337AD he was the leader of the Roman Empire. The evidence indicates that he saw in this newly forming institution a way to hold his vast empire together.

It is probable that Constantine became convinced that hope for the future lay in the determination and orderliness of Christianity, and that he wanted to enlist its growing strength in the service of the Empire. His aim in government was to preserve some form of unity, and it may have been partly for such reasons of policy that he accepted the Christian religion, (O'Grady, p. 75).

For a number of years before Constantine took the throne, the bishops had been having heated squabbles over the person of Christ—was He of the same essence as the Father, or was there a time He did not exist? In response to this in-fighting, Constantine:

> Needed Christianity to be doctrinally consistent and centrally organized if it was going to help him hold together the vast empire he had inherited. Hoping to create a strong sense of unity and cohesion among his subjects, he summoned some three hundred bishops...to a meeting in the Turkish city of Nicea, (Valantasis, p. xxii).

The Council of Nicea in 325AD "formulated a credo, a pledge that all Christians could recite that affirmed their basic beliefs," (Valantasis, p. xxii).

What happened here must be boldly underscored. A powerful civil ruler is calling "church leaders" together, and putting heavy pressure on them to come up with a statement that will significantly contribute to the unity of a worldly empire. "After the Council of Nicea, the imperially sanctioned and militarily supported separation of Christians into two camps, heretical and orthodox, began," (Valantasis, p. xxiv).

To illustrate how people gloss over historical realities in order to present an edited, rosy picture, consider a book for children, *The Story of St. Nicholas: More Than Reindeer and a Red Suit,* (Voice of the Martyrs, 2006).

> Later the evil Emperor Diocletian died, and a new emperor took the throne. His name was Constantine. He loved Jesus. So one day he issued an order, "Release all the Christians from prison!"... These songs [by Arius] began to cause many Christians to disagree about Jesus, so Emperor Constantine decided to have a meeting with all the church leaders in the Roman Empire.

It all sounds so nice, but the fundamental problems and evils are omitted.

Of course, the unity Constantine tried to create at Nicea failed miserably. Nevertheless, he kept asserting his authority by intervening in institutional "church" affairs in hopes of calming the theological storms.

> In his opinion, the Emperor, by virtue of his office, had the right to intervene in such controversies and to preside over the councils convened to settle them.... Constantine, himself, wanted to show that, by virtue of his Imperial office, he was supreme in ecclesiastical affairs, hoping thereby to mold the Church into an instrument for consolidating the absolute power of the Emperor, (O'Grady, p. 75).

The truth is, after the Council at Nicea there was a lot of confusion. Theological unanimity was a joke. Some exiled for their views were called back; some once viewed as heroes were exiled. All this had nothing to do with Christ. It was about raw human power and control.

> Doctrinal and personal quarrels multiplied and the Emperor intervened either to support or to exile the leaders of the conflicting parties. Three years after accepting the decrees of the Council of Nicea, Constantine changed his mind, recalled Arius from exile and supported the anti-Nicene party until the end of his reign, (O'Grady, p. 92).

Louis Berkhof noted that what happened at the Council of Nicea set the stage for the future:

> The decision of the Council did not terminate the controversy, but was rather only the beginning of it. A settlement forced upon the Church by the strong hand of the emperor could not satisfy and was also of uncertain duration. It made the determination of the Christian faith dependent on imperial caprice and even on court intrigues.... The sequel clearly proved that, as it was, a change in emperor, and altered mood, or even a bribe, might alter the whole aspect of the controversy. This is exactly what happened repeatedly in subsequent history, (*The History of Christian Doctrines*, Banner of Truth, 1978, p. 87).

Once the State was subsidizing this new entity called "church," the power of the bishops kept expanding.

> By the time Christianity became the official religion of the Empire, the power of the bishops had become enormous. In his diocese the bishop commanded almost supernatural prestige; he was the popular choice of the people and he now had official powers of jurisdiction over his clergy, and over any other case brought before him. Because the Church in the 4th Century, through this far-reaching power of the bishops, had become an indispensable part of the social welfare of the State, it seemed at times that it would even become an organ of the Imperial Government, (O'Grady, p. 77).

So, by 350AD the original vision of Jesus Christ was totally abandoned, and had been fully and officially replaced by a human organization calling itself "church," which had jumped into bed with the State. "The Church was taking Roman organization, philosophy and jurisprudence into its service," (O'Grady, p. 61). The church had become a worldly business, a bureaucracy, and was now consumed with preserving and perpetuating its religious accoutrements. As the Cardinal said to Christ in *Brothers Karamazov,* "We took from *him,* the wise and mighty spirit of the wilderness, what You rejected with scorn—Rome and the sword of Caesar."

ORGANIZED "ORTHODOXY"

We hear the word "orthodoxy" and generally think, "that which is right (orthodox) in contrast to that which is wrong (heterodox)." But it is just not that simple. Let's remember, the primary impetus to have "Christianity doctrinally consistent and centrally organized" *came from a self-aggrandizing emperor.* Constantine presided at the Council of Nicea in 325AD. Do you think the bishops could be objective about the issues before them with the Emperor sitting there? How many were exiled for giving the wrong answers?

An "Orthodoxy," in concrete, was being formed by bishops as ecclesiastical power was being centralized in Rome more and more, and civil emperors shaped the agenda for the newly established church. Those who questioned "orthodoxy," or stood outside of it, found themselves facing real dangers.

But, already in the fourth century, a persecuted Church had turned persecutor. Those who disagreed with 'orthodox' teachings were stripped of their authority and exiled. In one instance, when all persuasion had failed to bring the dissenters back into the fold, Church and State joined to put them down by force. These dissenters were the Donatists, (O'Grady, p. 79).

In the 4th Century the Emperor had the upper hand in church affairs. It came to be a deadly assumption that the civil leader would take the helm in theological matters.

So the institution by the Emperor of ecumenical councils was considered to be the act not of a political leader, but of the leader of the Christian people. The Emperor was automatically asked to intervene in theological arguments. The general councils were summoned and guided by imperial authority, (O'Grady, p. 90).

WRANGLING WITH WORDS AND EACH OTHER

The new visible church became a battle ground for one controversy after another. One Greek letter left in, or omitted, became the source of endless infighting. When the bishops should have put their hands over their mouths, they kept going on and on into areas of speculation to refute the "heretics."

The Greeks, who adopted the new religion, brought with them their love of disputation and logical definition, (O'Grady, p. 89). The attempt to combat Gnosticism with definitions was to give rise to further definitions, and then to further arguments about those definitions, and so to accusations and counter-accusations of heresy.... But once the questions were raised and other 'heretics' gave their response, it seemed that an official answer had to be given. It may have been necessary to have definitions, but it is possible that the very act of defining distorts the understanding of that which lies beyond logic, (O'Grady, p. 33).

In studying these controversies and the Councils that attempted to settle them, it often seems that their endless dissentions, condemnations and counter-condemnations were merely theologians' quarrels about the detailed use of words, and about minute differences in the 'expression of the inexpressible.' St. Hilary of Poitiers, writing to the Emperor Constantine complained that "Every year, nay every moon, we make new creeds to describe invisible Mysteries. We repent of what we have done, we defend those who repent, and we anathematize those whom we defended. We condemn either the doctrine of others in ourselves or our own in that of others; and, reciprocally tearing one another to pieces, we have been the cause of each other's ruin." (O'Grady, p. 89)

TAKEOVER OF THE CHURCH WAS ALWAYS ABOUT POWER AND CONTROL

With the narrowing definition of "orthodoxy," the "bishops demanded from their faithful" a "blind faith" and "mindless trust," (Valantasis, p. 126). From cradle to grave, the dark cloud of the institutional church hovered over them, packaged in seven "sacraments" and a labyrinth of other religious rituals and performance-based duties. Is it any wonder that when civil liberties emerged much later, people exited from the established churches? Henri Nouwen made these pointed observations:

> When I ask myself the main reason for so many people having left the church during the past decades in France, Germany, Holland, and also in Canada and America, the word *"power"* easily comes to mind. One of the greatest ironies of the history of Christianity is that its leaders constantly gave in to the temptation of power—political power, military power, economic power, or moral and spiritual power—even though they continued to speak in the name of Jesus, who did not cling to his divine power but emptied himself and became as we are. We keep hearing from others, as well as saying to ourselves, that having power—provided it is used in the service of God and your fellow human beings—is a good thing. With this rationalization, crusades took place; inquisitions were organized; Indians were enslaved; positions of great influence were desired; episcopal palaces, splendid cathedrals, and opulent seminaries were built; and much moral manipulation of conscience was engaged in. Every time we see a major crisis in the history of the church, such as the Great Schism of the eleventh century, the Reformation of the sixteenth century, or the immense secularization of the twentieth century, we always see that a major cause of rupture is the power exercised by those who claim to be followers of the poor and powerless Jesus, (H. Nouwen, *In the Name of Jesus*, pp. 75-77).

> Power offers an easy substitute for the hard task of love. It seems easier to be God than to love God, easier to control people than to love people, easier to own life than to love life. Jesus asks, "Do you love me?" We ask, "Can we sit at your right hand and your left hand in your Kingdom?", (H. Nouwen, *In the Name of Jesus*, p. 77).

> The long painful history of the church is the history of people ever and again tempted to choose power over love, control over the cross, being a leader over being led, (H. Nouwen, *In the Name of Jesus*, pp. 78-79).

> One thing is clear to me: The temptation of power is greatest when intimacy is feared. Much Christian leadership is exercised by people who do not know how to develop healthy, intimate relationships and have opted for power and control instead. Many Christian empire builders have been people unable to give and receive love, (H. Nouwen, *In the Name of Jesus*, p. 79).

AN EXAMPLE OF "OUTSIDE THE BOX"

"Montanus was the male founder" of a movement, and he "began to prophesy in Phrygia, in Asia Minor (modern Turkey) sometime around 170AD," (Valantasis, p. 100).

This "group of Christians who broke away from the main Church in the second half of the second century were the Montanists...they sought a return to the purity of original Christianity, declaring that the rules governing the ethical behavior of Christians were not given through the authority of bishops and Church institutions, but by God alone, speaking through the inspired prophets.... His [Montanus] declared mission was to bring about a return to the simplicity of the early Church, and to announce the fulfillment of the prophecy of Pentecost." (O'Grady, p. 60)

"Montanus called forth a vision of a church renewed—filled with the Holy Spirit, alive with fresh prophecy, and eagerly awaiting the imminent return of Christ," (Valantasis, p. 100). "The Montanists...aimed at a freer, more emotional form of religion," (O'Grady, p. 60).

Women fully participated in this movement, (Valantasis, p. 102). "Woman after woman, then man after man, would channel words from God, while the others listened attentively," (Valantasis, p. 99).

"The Montanists understood their new prophecy as a renewal movement for an increasingly decadent church," (Valantasis, p. 101).

They did not challenge the Constantinian church's sacramental and hierarchical system, (Valantasis, p. 102). "Their fervency for reform did not extend to their church's structure," and thus they ordained women and men as "deacons, presbyters (priests) and bishops," (Valantasis, pp. 103, 102). "The famous North African Latin theologian Tertullian, 160 – 225AD, converted to the movement and wrote energetically from a Montanist perspective," (Valantasis, p. 105).

My purpose here is not to defend or condemn what the Montanists practiced. Rather, it is to underscore that this "outside the box" group deeply disturbed those in power within the "orthodox church." "Obviously the leadership of the [main] church could not have people claiming to channel the divine voice directly...and so the Montanists eventually were excommunicated," (Valantasis, p. 104).

"Mysticism in an organization leads to a crisis of authority, and many of the internal disputes of the first three centuries of the Christian church concerned the problem of revelations," (Fanning, p. 19).

"The reaction of the anti-Montanist Christians indicates that the mainstream of Christianity no longer experienced possession by the Holy Spirit as a normative feature of the faith.... The promise of the unmediated, indwelling divinity within the believer offered a means of bypassing the authority of the emerging hierarchy of bishops.... Moreover, the prominence of the prophetesses was considered to be unseemly by the male clergy," (Fanning, pp. 20-21).

The members of the religion had to be watchful of anything "that challenged in any manner the authority of the ecclesiastical leaders, or of its increasingly specific and narrowing orthodox faith." (Fanning, p. 21) As I.M. Lewis put it, "direct claim to divine knowledge is always a threat to the established order," (Fanning, p. 21).

By the 4th Century "there was a conflict between those who saw Christianity as a religion of the mind, a system of beliefs about God that was governed by the Scriptures, and those who saw Christianity as an experience of God," (Fanning, p. 34).

The Montanists vividly illustrate what would happen to any group in the future—like the Donatists—who pursued things in a different way, outside of the "orthodox" hierarchy.

DID CHRIST BUILD THIS MESS?

I have given above a concise, condensed summary of some key characteristics of the post-apostolic church:

1. That bishops became very powerful, and submission to God was equated with submission to them

2. That civil rulers became the controlling factor in the institutional church's affairs

3. That a central church hierarchy and a doctrinal system called "orthodoxy" were put into place in order to control peoples' lives

4. That those outside of the hierarchy and "orthodoxy" were viewed as "heretics" who were harassed and often killed

5. That in all these matters and more, what began when Christ came to the *ekklesia* in the Spirit on the Day of Pentecost was long lost after 150AD in a growing ecclesiastical bureaucracy

Now, I have a critical question for you to consider. But before the question, I want to set before you a little snapshot of "church life" in the 5th Century.

A Council was summoned at Ephesus in 431AD. The city mob demonstrated violently against the 'opponents of the Mother of God.' The Emperor intervened, and, at one time during the proceedings, imprisoned both Cyril *and* Nestorius. Churchmen condemned each other; the common people rioted; the Imperial civil servants carried on intrigues between both parties. Finally, [Emperor] Theodosius dismissed the Council saying, quite rightly, that it had failed to achieve reconciliation. But Nestorius himself was condemned as a heretic, deposed and exiled, (O'Grady, p. 103).

So, here we have the very strange situation where "church" then consisted of Emperors changing their theological views pragmatically, depending on various circumstances, and "bishops changed sides according to who was Emperor," (O'Grady, p. 106). Keep in mind that "three years after accepting the decrees of the Council of Nicea, Constantine changed his mind, recalled Arius from exile and supported the anti-Nicene party until the end of his reign,'" (O'Grady, p. 92).

The vital question, then, is this: *are you prepared to equate Christ's words, "I will build My ekklesia," with what called itself "church" from 300 – 1500AD?* And further, do we really believe that Christ was the Architect of this monstrous Institution? Did He build this religious bureaucracy or did humans who were craving for power and control?

I know this: *Christ has always been building His ekklesia,* but not in organizations that are intertwined with State power, not in organizations that depend on State support and backing for their existence, and not in organizations that murder people "outside the box" in Jesus' name.

What happened in 451AD in those riotous mobs, in those theological fights, and in the Emperor's hovering presence at the Council was not Christ. It was flesh, it was human control, and it was raw power.

Just because an institution calls itself "Church" does not mean it has anything to do with Christ. We need to come to terms with this reality. When Jesus builds something, it is Spirit, and it is Love. Further, Christ builds out of weakness, not fleshly power and control. As Nouwen put it so well:

> Power offers an easy substitute for the hard task of love. It seems easier to be God than to love God, easier to control people than to love people, easier to own life than to love life. Jesus asks, "Do you love me?" We ask, "Can we sit at your right hand and your left hand in your Kingdom?" The long, painful history of the church is the history of people ever and again tempted to choose power over love, control over the cross, being a leader over being led, (H. Nouwen, *In the Name of Jesus*, pp. 77, 78, 79).

Leonard Verduin in 1964 captured the tragedy and travesty that occurred in the post-apostolic church:

> The "fall" of the Church had so changed the visage of the Bride of Christ as to make her unrecognizable. She who had been sent on a mission of healing and helping had taken on the features of the modern police state, (*The Reformers and their Stepchildren*, p. 45; see p. 121).

In 1934, Alexander B. Macdonald noted the shift that took place from the first generation of believers to the ensuing centuries of the post-apostolic church:

> It should never be forgotten that even this great Apostolic Church was unable to maintain itself, for much longer than a single generation, upon the high levels of a free, spontaneous, Spirit-controlled worship, and by the end of the century was quite definitely moving down towards those less exalted levels on which the Church has lived and moved ever since, (*Christian Worship in the Primitive Church*, Edinburgh: T & T Clark, 1934, p. 9).

"It is a movement away from the state of things implied in 1 Corinthians – where pre-eminence in the Church depends on the personal possession of some spiritual gift (of which 'government' is one of the least esteemed) – and towards a state of things where importance is attached to the holding of an office invested with recognized authority."

—**B.H. Streeter,** *The Primitive Church,* p. 83; cited in Alexander B. Macdonald, *Christian Worship in the Primitive Church,* T & T Clark, p. 71

CHAPTER 5
WHO'S IN CHARGE? A LOOK AT AUTHORITY

WHAT "CHURCH" LEADERS SAY:

"The pastor is not only the authoritative communicator of the truth from the Head to the Body, but he is also the accurate communicator of the needs from the Body to the Head," (David L. McKenna, 1980).

"The pastor has the power in a growing church.... The pastor of a growing church may appear to outsiders as a dictator. But to the people of the church, his decisions are their decisions," (C. Peter Wagner, 1976).

"An orderly church needs one overseer, one shepherd, one pastor.... The pastor needs to have general oversight of the education, music, youth, activities and any other ministries in a flock.... Allow this old veteran to observe that chaos easily develops where no one is in charge. If the church is to be one flock, it needs one shepherd,"(Frank Owen, 1981).

"God-called pastors...have authority over the assemblies. Other Christians are to submit to this authority. As a church member, pastor-elders are over me in the Lord. When I honor and submit to them, I am not submitting merely to a man; I am submitting to the Lord and Chief Shepherd of the church.... The deacon is a servant of the pastor.... [A pastor] must have the final decision concerning what is taught and by whom, and must judge all things that are taught to make certain it is correct.... A pastor doesn't need permission from the deacons or the lead families of the church in regard to who he invites to preach or what Sunday School lessons to use, etc.... A pastor can have his way in the church in this present world even if he is wrong and sinning, because there is no higher earthly ecclesiastical authority in the assembly.... Don't give your authority to those who are not pastors, such as deacons, and don't allow strong men or women to control things from "behind the scenes".... If I am not a pastor, why would God lead me in regard to how the church is operated instead of leading the pastor?... Don't confuse your job with that of the pastor. As a non-pastor, you don't have the authority of the pastor nor do you have the work of the pastor (visiting the sick, burying dead, being on call for any need, watching for souls, the care of the church, bearing the brunt of the devil's attack against the church). You also do not have the responsibility of the pastor." (David Cloud, http://www. wayoflife.org/database/pastorsauthority.html)

"The Elder (Pastor) Board is final authority in all spiritual and temporal matters," (*Constitution,* Faith Bible Church, Canton, Ohio).

"Shepherds lead sheep, the sheep do not lead the shepherd!... Many problems arise in churches where men of the congregation assume authority that belongs in the pastor's arena.... 'Obey them that have the rule over you and submit yourselves,' and that word has the meaning of a willing submission unto the authority that has been delegated to pastors.... When a congregation has the attitude, 'We will run things around here, Pastor. You just preach to us,' they are saying, in essence, 'We don't submit to your rule as pastor.' Any church, or church member, who rebels against the biblical rule of a pastor, is rebelling against God, not that pastor.... The congregation is to obey the pastor.... He rules over them, leads them, and instructs them. They are to submit willingly to his rule and leadership.... 'That is not your business, that is the business of the superintendent.' I reminded him that as pastor I was the overseer of the superintendent, the teachers and every other aspect of the church's work. There is no area of a church's work that is not under the oversight of the pastor.... No church should engage in anything that the pastor cannot oversee. If it would be wrong for him to oversee it, it would be wrong for the church to do it!" (Wayne Camp, http://www.gpp-5grace. com/pastor.htm)

"A pastor has authority over the church and so no woman, according to Scripture, is to be over a man in authority in the church or at home (Eph 5:24)."   (http://www.whatchristianswanttoknow.com/should-women-be-pastors-or-elders-of-a-church-a-bible-study/#ixzz2bDhjhhiA)

THE BUSINESS EQUIVALENT IS:

Pastor = CEO

Deacon Board = Board of Directors

Voting Members = Shareholders

I know a lot of people are uncomfortable with comparing churches and businesses. But that's the way things work. (http://www.freerepublic.com/focus/religion/3022486/posts)

WHAT THE NEW TESTAMENT SAYS:

There are numerous layers of misconceptions and erroneous teachings about "authority" in the hierarchical religious system. In fact, there are so many wrong assumptions that one might despair of knowing where to start in displaying reality about this subject. We must start by looking closely at how the primary word for "authority" is actually used in the New Testament.

Exousia is the most-used word for "authority." It is used 105 times in the NT. Here is the breakdown in terms of occurrences of how the *exousia* is used.

- Authority of Jesus – 39 times
- Authority of heavenly and earthly rulers – 31 times
- Authority given by Father or Christ to believers – 15 times
- Authority of Father – 6 times
- Authority of Satan – 5 times
- Authority of Jewish religious leaders – 4
- Authority of the darkness – 2
- Authority of the believing wife – 1
- Authority of the believing husband – 1
- Non-authority of the second death – 1

How many times have you heard people say things like, "Parental authority must be used to train children," and "We must be careful not to infringe on the pastor's authority"? People connect "authority" to all kinds of so-called church-related offices and ministries. This makes it all the more striking that *exousia* is nowhere in the N.T. specifically connected to:

1. Husbands over wives

2. Parents over children

3. Elders/overseers/pastors and deacons over an *ekklesia*

The point is that in the midst of all the banter about the word "authority," nowhere in the N.T. is it used with reference to any person or persons being "over" other believers.

The only place in the N.T. where "authority" is linked to marriage has nothing to do with "male headship." The verb form, *exousiazo* (to have authority over), is used twice in 1 Corinthians 7:1-5 concerning the marriage relationship. However, here it has nothing to do with a husband's alleged authority over a wife, but rather a mutual authority over each other's body. The couple is not to separate from each other for a season without "symphony"—mutual consent.

The traditional concept of the husband's "headship" has meant, "Be the head (final decision-maker) of the wife," (P.B. Wilson, p. 69). How can this notion be squared with what Paul said in 1 Corinthians 7:1-5? According to the traditional approach, the husband could rightfully say, "As the final decision-maker, Honey, I'm going away for a month to seek the Lord." But Paul asserted that the couple should only separate for a while if both parties agree and are in "symphony." Hardly sounds like the husband is the "final" decision-maker! Based on how the word "authority" *(exousia)* is used in the New Testament, let's make some crucial observations:

1. Which human or humans have "authority" in the *ekklesia* is a non-issue in the N.T. because *it is clear that all authority resides in Jesus Christ.* Jesus

has authority over all people in order that He can give eternal life to each one that the Father has given Him, (John 17:2).

2. In contexts where authority is "given" to humans, it has nothing to do with being "over" other people. Rather, it has to do with overcoming things like disease, evil spirits, and death. The importance of this point must be underscored. From what is expressed in the quotations above from church leaders, you can see that they have wrongly connected authority with an official position that places them in charge of the people in the pews. This practice is completely out of touch with Jesus' words, "not so among you."

In light of our look at the shape "authority" takes in the New Testament, it seems clear that we need to re-visit just about everything we've ever learned about this topic, and jettison many assumptions we've accepted that really have no foundation in Christ.

Church history reveals that early on "authority" was disjoined from Christ and put into the hands of men whose driving force was to control people—mostly using fear, threats and coercion—and to keep them under their thumbs. The history of authority in the visible church has left a bloody trail of carnage and death. Whenever the aroma of the foot-washing Christ is snuffed out, power-hungry church leaders will fill the religious vacuum.

A people out of whom are flowing the living waters of Christ's shared life have no time to waste, or energy to expend, about "Who is in charge?" on the human level. They know, as Milt Rodriguez exclaimed, "Christ is large and He is in charge!" Authority comes from Christ, and is expressed through each and every part of His Bride, for Christ is in them with life.

For Further Reflection:

Walter L. Liefield, "The Nature of Authority in the New Testament," *Discovering Biblical Equality,* Ronald W. Pierce, and Rebecca Merrill Groothuis, general editors; Gordon D. Fee, contributing editor, IVP, 2004.

CHAPTER 6

THE ORIGIN OF THE FLOW—A LOOK AT "HEAD"

Words are tricky. They have histories, so their meanings can change as generations roll by. They have contexts, and thus their meanings can be nuanced. There are writers who use them in peculiar ways. All these factors, and others, certainly come into play with the Greek word *kephale* ("head").

As is the case with the word "authority," the word "head" has many clutching barnacles attached to it that muddy the waters. P.B. Wilson expresses the typical view of "head" in words addressed to husbands: "Be the head (final decision maker) of the wife" (*Liberated Through Submission*, p. 69). More often than not, then, the word "head" is assumed to mean "authority over" someone, usually the wife.

We have inherited the concept of "chief decision-maker" connected to the word "head." But, we need to understand that in the 1st Century; it was thought that the *viscera* (gut) was the decision-making center, not the *head* (Linda Belleville, "What the English Translators Aren't Telling You," 2003). So, for us now to assume that "head" in the N.T. means main decision-maker gets us off on the wrong foot from the get-go.

The revelation in the N.T. will not sustain the traditional viewpoint of "authority over" and "decision-maker." Let's look at the specifics of the Greek word *kephale* ("head").

Kephale is used 76 times in the New Testament.

Kephale refers to the physical head of persons or beings 61 times.

Kephale is used in a non-literal sense 15 times:

1. Christ as the "head" of every husband (1 Cor. 11)

2. The husband as the "head" of the wife (1 Cor. 11)

3. The "head" of Christ is God (1 Cor. 11)

4. Christ is "head" over everything for the *ekklesia's* sake (Eph. 1:22)

5. Christ as the "head" of His body on earth (Eph. 4:15)

6. The husband as the "head" of his wife just as Christ is the "Head" of the *ekklesia* (Eph. 5:23)

7. Christ as the "Head" of the body, the *ekklesia* (Col. 1:18)

8. Christ as the "Head" of all principalities & powers (Col. 2:10)

9. Error flows out of not holding Christ as the "Head," from whom the *ekklesia* is nourished (Col. 2:19)

10. Five times in the N.T. (Matthew 21:42, Mark 12:10, Luke 20:17, Acts 4:11 and 1 Peter 2:7) Jesus is said to be "the Head of the corner," which comes from Psalm 118:22. This concept is also found in Ephesians 2:20 where Christ is called the "chief cornerstone," but the word *kephale* is not used here (see Isaiah 28:16)

With two possible exceptions (Eph. 1:22, Col. 2:10), the overwhelming sense of *kephale* is "source/origin," indicating an organic/relational setting. We use the word in this sense when we speak of the place where a river begins as "the headwaters," or origin of the flow.

For example, think of Adam and Eve in Eden. Adam was her "head" in the sense that she was taken out of him. This was, as Paul noted, all about Christ and the *ekklesia* (Eph. 5:32). The *ekklesia* was "in Christ" before the foundation of the world, and in His death, burial and resurrection. She was, as it were, birthed from His side as a glorious Bride.

There was nothing in the pristine garden to indicate that Adam had "authority over" Eve. Rather, the pre-fall language speaks of partnership—"He gave *them* dominion"—"He called *them* Adam."

Thus, in 1 Corinthians 11, when Paul said that the man is not out of the woman, but the woman out of the man, etc., his conclusion of mutuality in verses 11-12 must not be missed—"nevertheless, neither woman without man nor man without woman *in the Lord*. For as the woman is of the man, even so is the man also through woman; but all things of God." The adversative "nevertheless," Gordon Fee points out, "seems clearly designed to keep the earlier argument from being read in a subordinationist way," (*NICNT: The First Epistle to the Corinthians*, Eerdmans, 1987, p. 524).

As a side note, it is of interest that several post-apostolic theologians around 400AD—Cyril and Chrysostom—did not view "head" in 1 Corinthians 11 as "authority over." Cyril saw "source": "the head of the woman is man, because she was taken from his flesh." Chrysostom said, "If you think 'head' means 'chief' or 'boss,' you skew the Godhead," (Jon Zens, *What's With Paul & Women*, p. 131). The fact that they made this observation is noteworthy because in their other writings they frequently denigrated women.

The image in Colossians 2:19 is clearly organic, not chain-of-command. "Hold to the Head, from Whom the whole body will grow with the growth of God." This echoes Jesus' words in John 15, "I am the Vine, you are the branches—abide in Me and you will bear fruit."

Reflect on Ephesians 5:21-22 for a moment. First, Paul told all believers to mutually submit to one another. Then he said, "Wives to your own husbands." There is no verb, so one must draw it from verse 21—"wives [submit] to your own husbands." Then it is stated that Christ is the "Head" of the *ekklesia,* and that the husband is the "head" of the wife. Does a military, chain-of-command, "authority over" picture fit here? Of course not. The image is organic and relational. Just as Christ is the Source of the *ekklesia,* so the husband as the source is to cherish and nourish his wife. (Notice that in Eph. 5:22-33, the bulk of what is presented is directed toward husbands, not wives.)

In the five citations of Psalm 118:22 where *kephale* is used as "head of the corner," the sense is Christ as the foundation and plumb line. Obviously, these five examples are central in the N.T. use of the word. The image here has nothing to do with "authority over" something. It is an architectural picture.

We have seen in our examination of Jesus' non-hierarchical teachings about relationships that there is no place for any brother or sister to be "in authority over" others. Jesus' kingdom is *relational* and *organic,* not a military chain-of-command. Putting "head" in a living Vine-branch setting helps us to perceive that, with few exceptions, "Source" is a better translation of *kephale* than "supreme over."

The use of the word "head" in the N.T. politely forces us to make a decision: *are we going to pursue relationships in the body of Christ (like marriage) in a cold, military, chain-of-command way, or in an organic, mutual and relational way?*

Christ is not the "Head," the General, of a military force barking orders to His troops. No, He is the Loving Source of cherishing and nourishing life for all of His sheep.

For Further Reflection:

Linda L. Belleville, "Κεφαλη and the Thorny Issue of Headcovering in 1 Corinthians 11:2-6." *Paul and the Corinthians: Studies on a Community in Conflict. Essays in Honor of Margaret Thrall,* edited by Trevor J. Burke and J. Keith Elliott. Leiden/Boston: Brill, 2003.

Doxa.ws has some excellent material on "Head" in the NT. While the content is very helpful, the articles are not "clean," in the sense that there are many typos, grammatical errors, and sometimes the presentation is choppy (some parts may be translated from another language?).

http://www.doxa.ws/social/Women/women_index.html

    www.doxa.ws/social/Women/head.html
    www.doxa.ws/social/Women/head2.html
    www.doxa.ws/social/Women/head3.html
    www.doxa.ws/social/Women/veil2.html

Laurie Fasullo, *What about the word Kephale ("head") in the New Testament?* http://www.searchingtogether.org/kephale.htm

Gordon D. Fee, "Praying and Prophesying in the Assemblies: 1 Corinthians 11:2-16," *Discovering Biblical Equality,* Ronald W. Pierce, and Rebecca Merrill Groothuis, general editors; Gordon D. Fee, contributing editor, IVP, 2004, pp. 142-160

J. Lee Grady, "The Dark Side of Wives Submitting to Husbands," August 7, 2013. http://www.charismamag.com/blogs/fire-in-my-bones/7229-the-dark-side-of-submission

CHAPTER 7

GOD'S PURPOSE IN CHRIST LIVED OUT AMONG PORCUPINES: LIVING OUT THE TENSION OF THE BEAUTIES OF CHRIST AND THE REALITIES OF LIFE WITH ONE ANOTHER

Years ago, Vernon Grounds wrote an article about "the fellowship of porcupines." He noted that all of us are capable of poking one another in hurtful ways. The DNA of Christ in us longs for a community of shared life in Christ. But, as Henri Nouwen observed, the path to vibrant community "is hard and full of difficulties," (H. Nouwen, *Reaching Out,* p. 46).

From the Lord's perspective and purpose, He birthed the *ekklesia* on earth to express and display His Son. And through the *ekklesia,* He makes His wisdom known to the principalities and powers that rule in the heavenlies, thereby, His reign and love in the *ekklesia* will be seen by the watching world, (Ephesians 3:10; John 13:35).

Thus, despite the numerous obstacles and challenges to a believing community, fully functioning *ekklesia* is not optional, but the vitality and the heart of God's eternal purpose in Christ. Followers of Christ on earth are faced with living in a serious tension within the messiness of His family, yet nevertheless, continuing to pursue Him together as those captured by His eternal purpose for His Son to have a Bride.

Nouwen crisply captured the essence of community when he called it "a joyful togetherness of spontaneous people," (H. Nouwen, *Reaching Out,* p. 15). Wouldn't many of us be thrilled—even delirious—if we could be part of a Jesus community that pulses with the Son's life as expressed in this summary of how some African tribes function?

> Community is the spirit, the guiding light of the tribe, whereby people come together in order to fulfill a specific purpose, to help others fulfill

their purpose, and to take care of one another. The goal of community is to make sure that each member of the community is heard and is properly giving the gifts he/she has brought to this world. Without this giving, the community dies. And without the community, the individual is left without a place where he can contribute. The community is that grounding place where people come and share their gifts and receive from others, (*The Spirit of Intimacy: Ancient African Teachings in the Ways of Relationships,* Sobonfu Some, Quill, 2000, p. 22).

So why do we find it so difficult to live the shared life of Christ with others? Why does a believing community seem to blossom so infrequently? I think it would be beneficial to touch upon some of the formidable challenges that we must wrestle with in the context of community.

CULTURAL QUILLS

Every culture has its peculiar characteristics that give believers a sure test of faith as they follow Jesus. Here are four to reflect upon.

1. *Mobility:* In our era, mobility is an issue in most places in the world. But in America it seems that many people are too mobile! Folks do not remain in the same place long enough to establish community with other believers. They are always moving for a variety of reasons. This makes it not only difficult, but near impossible to develop community together. Usually the parting takes place before the bond of Christ takes root through knowing Him in and through one another.

2. *Distance:* Many Americans drive long distances one-way from home to the church building of their choice. The fact remains that deepening relationships cannot be built from a distance. Living within reasonable proximity to one another facilitates community Life. Authentic community is the everyday things and everyday life that we share together.

3. *Individualism:* We live in a culture where, for the most part, people have built walls around themselves, and they don't want to let any body in. People live in subdivisions and have never met their neighbors. "Jeremy Seabrook refers to the 'strangers who live where neighborhoods once were'.... It may be stated strongly that we have witnessed a striking increase in the sense of separate, differentiated identity and a corresponding sharp decline in the sense of community and belonging," (Paul L. Wachtel, "America, Land of Lost Community," *Searching Together,* 38:3-4, 2012, p. 29).

   Given that believers have usually been infected with forms of individualism, it takes a fresh revelation from Christ in order for them to see that in the Spirit they are part of a Body in which they receive from and give to the other parts, (1 Cor. 12:13).

4. *Materialism and Consumerism:* Most Americans feel pressured to devote a lot of time to obtaining and maintaining their things and their career. Building Christ-centered communities will involve each follower re-visiting how they use their time, money and resources. Community flows out of believers giving priority to Christ in others, not to pouring time and resources into things that will perish. Bruce Springsteen captured the spirit of this in "Blood Brothers":

> We played king of the mountain out on the end
> The world come chargin' up the hill, and we were women and men
> Now there's so much that time, time and memory fade away
> We got our own roads to ride and chances we gotta take
> We stood side by side, each one fightin' for the other
> We said until we died, we'd always be blood brothers

> Now the hardness of this world slowly grinds your dreams away
> Makin' a fool's joke out of the promises we make
> And what once seemed black and white turns to so many shades of gray
> We lose ourselves in work to do and bills to pay
> And it's a ride, ride, ride, and there ain't much cover
> With no one runnin' by your side my blood brother

It is with great sadness that we must observe that the churches people see on the street corners are not *counter-cultural,* but for the most part they acquiesce to American cultural norms. Is it any wonder that we do not see the Life of Christ in believers coming to expression in vital community? The very church structures themselves—both the buildings and the hierarchy—tend to foster *mobility* (people hopping from one church to the next), *distance* (relationships are not developed), *individualism* (no cultivation of body-life), and *materialism/consumerism* (church budgets need so much to pay for the buildings, the upkeep, their image, and the salaries).

PERSONAL QUILLS

If we have the privilege of entering into developing community life, then each of us will bring our personal baggage into the group. It is inevitable. So, not only do we face cultural issues that hinder community, we also have internal battles that can affect the expression of community.

1. *Toxic Personalities:* This is a huge topic, but here I would like to address three common manifestations. The first is the person who has a *beginning vision of what organic ekklesia is about, yet has a toxic personality.* This person has read many books, listened to mp3's, been to conferences, and expresses a longing for "New Testament body-life." The reality is, however, that if such a person tried to become part of a developing group, they might very well destroy it.

Thomas Dubay observed that "possibly the most thorny obstacle to successful dialoging is the 'problem person.' The individual we have in mind is hypercritical of almost everything except what he/she favors and does. He/

she has a domineering manner that tends to crush 'the opposition'.... his/her tongue is sharp and he/she often hurts others with it. What can a community do? This person usually has a personal psychological problem, though they indignantly deny the mere suggestion. He/she most likely needs professional help. [Care must be taken] that this person does not destroy the community's relationships and efforts at communication. If kindly admonitions bear no fruit, he/she should be excluded from dialog sessions," ("Communication in Community," *Searching Together*, 14:4, 1985, p. 10).

Interacting with such people is a delicate matter. On the one hand, we cannot set up a mental health hoop for folks to jump through, as if all their ducks must be in a row; we all have a few ducks awry. As Nouwen pointed out, "The act on the stage of our life will probably always look better than what goes on behind the curtains, but as long as we are willing to face the contrast, and struggle to minimize it, the tension can keep us humble by allowing us to offer our service to others, without being whole ourselves," (H. Nouwen, *Reaching Out*, p. 50).

Believing communities must be therapeutic—that is, "they assist members to grow to the fullness of their life in Christ," (Hammett/Sofield, "Developing Healthy Christian Community," *Searching Together*, 24:3, 1996, p. 4). We must come along side one another in order to participate in the process of mutual healing.

We all need to ask ourselves, "Given the fact that everyone has shortcomings, are my behavior patterns such that I might tear a group apart, instead of building it up?" We may know what is in the books, and we may have heard the conference speakers, but are we honestly prepared to enter into deeper relationships with other brothers and sisters? Are we willing to prefer others ahead of ourselves? Do we need help from the Body of Christ, or other sources, before we dive into authentic body life?

2. *The Utopian Personality:* The next person is the one who *has a vision for Christ-centered ekklesia and is now seeking to find that near-perfect, "Biblical" expression of it.* "People suffering from loneliness," Nouwen points out, "often deepened by the lack of affection in their intimate family circle, search for a final solution for their pains, and look at a new friend, a new lover or a new community with Messianic expectations," (H. Nouwen, *Reaching Out*, p. 19).

After a short time of searching for an unrealistic experience of body life, such a person will usually succumb to disappointment and frustration due to the impractical and unfulfilled expectations that he/she has put upon the body. Often, the result displays itself with emotional reactions that are accompanied by anger, anxiety, aggression and cynicism toward other members of the body. Such a person has the potential to obstruct or hinder the expression of

Christ through the *ekklesia*. Another important aspect is that such a person creates a dissatisfied and disgruntled atmosphere, which adversely affects the relationships that have already been established.

> To wait for moments or places where no pain exists, no separation is felt, and where all human restlessness has turned into inner peace is waiting for a dream world. No friend or lover, no husband or wife, no community or commune will be able to put to rest our deepest cravings for unity and wholeness, (H. Nouwen, *Reaching Out*, p. 19).

Exalting unreachable utopian ideals may even have another tragic side effect: "By burdening others with these divine expectations...we might inhibit the expression of free friendship and love, and evoke instead feelings of inadequacy and weakness. Friendship and love cannot develop in the form of an anxious clinging to each other," (H. Nouwen, *Reaching Out*, p. 19).

It is right for us to pursue with passion the Lord's purposes in building His house, but we must always remember that His *ekklesia* on earth is not a conflict-free utopia, but rather more like a hospital with many healing rooms.

3. *The Leader Personality:* The third type of person is the one *who has been accustomed to being a leader for varying periods of time, or covets the leadership role, and then assumes that he/she will continue or take on this role in a small-group setting.* Bringing this mind-set into a group that meets outside the institutional church is devastating. This problem has probably more often been the ruin of communities than any other.

People who for years have filled the preconceived leadership roles found in traditional churches and now find themselves outside the system must reassess their functioning in the body of Christ. Instead of assuming to be a "leader," they must learn how to be "just a brother or sister." Of course, this is not usually easy to pull off. Nouwen pinpoints several key heart perspectives for those coming out of traditional leadership positions: "Jesus has a different vision of maturity: It is the ability and willingness to be led where you would not rather go.... [to be] led to unknown, undesirable, and painful places.... Jesus promises a life in which we increasingly have to stretch our hands and be led to places where we would rather not go.... The long painful history of the church is the history of people ever and again tempted to choose power over love, control over the cross, being a leader over being led, (H. Nouwen, *In the Name of Jesus*, pp. 81-82, 91, 79).

If a group meeting in a living room begins its life together by looking to a "former" church leader to start the meeting, choose some songs, do the teaching, and generally be the go-to person—that community is already doomed. Large doses of two great books would be of great benefit—*Reimagining Church* and *Finding Organic Church* by Frank Viola.

RELATIONAL QUILLS

Of the many important matters that could be pursued here, I would like to touch on two—one from the general perspective of the "new humanity," and the other a specific type of person that is troublesome.

A PLACE OF LOVE AND DIVERSITY

Just think for a moment about the sociological radicalness of the early church. There were Jews and Gentiles, men, women and children, slaves and free, poor folks and those with more, the illiterate and those with more education—*all in one place, eating and drinking of Christ together.* Such a diverse configuration of people was unknown in Jesus' and Paul's day.

Picture yourself in a 1st Century gathering with 25 folks from pagan and synagogue backgrounds. It would have been easy and convenient for the developing early church to divide along ethnic lines. It could have been suggested, "Why don't those schooled in the Torah meet at Solomon's home, and those from the nations meet at Aurelius' house?"

That could have been done, but such actions would have contradicted everything Jesus died for, (see: Gal. 2:11-21). The cross, made the two—Jewish and Gentile believers—*into a new humanity,* where the brothers and sisters did not relate to one another in terms of worldly distinctions (rich/poor, male/female, etc.), but in the reality of the Living Christ dwelling in each unique person.

Just think of all the practical issues that had to be worked out in the 1st Century between very different people groups in light of Romans 14 and 15. Just eating together required a deep love and sensitivity for each other. The Jews looked at the Gentiles as "dogs," outside the covenant promises. The Gentiles viewed the Jews as a very peculiar people with many strange scruples. Yet "in Christ" they are now all gathered around a table together, feasting on Christ who brought them together.

This is what Francis Schaeffer called "sociological healing." We must never forget that the *horizontal* dimension of Christ's cross is just as real and vital as the *vertical* dimension in which He died for our sins. Historically, the God-ward (vertical) aspect has received the bulk of attention, while the one-another (horizontal) has gone largely undeveloped.

LOOK AT MY SLEEVE

One of the most frequent challenges to community is the person who feels compelled to display all of their convictions prominently on their sleeve. In any human encounter—whether one-on-one or in a group—such an individual can't let an opportunity pass to let others know his/her opinion on a wide range of issues.

We have all had such people cross our path. But if we are honest, I believe most of us would confess to having been guilty of this problem for varying periods in our lives. Henri Nouwen gives us a glimpse of this type of person.

> Someone who is filled with ideas, concepts, opinions and convictions cannot be a good host. There is no inner space to listen, no openness to discover the gift of the other. It is not difficult to see how those "who know

it all" can kill a conversation and prevent an interchange of ideas, (H. Nouwen, *Reaching Out,* p. 74).

It usually does not take long to spot such a person, because right away when a conversation begins, they will announce such things as—"Most Bible versions are compromised; the King James is the best"—"That big earthquake that happened the other day is sure proof that we are in the last days, close to the rapture—"Those Democrats are sure flushing our country down the toilet, aren't they?"—"Yeah, I'm a vegetarian; research shows that's the best way to eat"— "It's a shame how many businesses are open on Sunday these days"—"I can't believe that Christians can bring Christmas trees into their homes."

We all need to be a whole lot more cautious about how we parade our convictions in front of others—especially around people that we do not know, or are getting to know. *Our convictions and scruples are not Christ, they are our preferences.* The antidote for the sleeve-syndrome is a fuller revelation of Jesus Christ. When we are around other people, Christ must be our passion, not our peculiar notions of politics or other raging cultural or religious issues.

To the extent that Jesus Christ increases in a believing community, sleeve-issues will recede, diminish and vanish. Folks consumed with Jesus will have no time to be distracted by prophecy charts and survivalist schemes.

Without question, there are numerous *cultural, personal and relational obstacles* to robust believing community. Should we, then, give up and throw in the towel? Certainly some do, but I would suggest that it is the Lord's intention to fuel our hearts with a revelation of His passion for the Son and His Bride.

IS IT WORTH THE BATTLE?

Paul certainly could have composed a list of reasons why he could just quit and walk away from laying the foundation of Christ everywhere he went. He was misunderstood, criticized, maligned and bore the marks of Christ's sufferings on his body. But the one key truth that kept him going day-after-day was *God's eternal purpose in Christ finding ongoing expression in the ekklesia on earth.* This vision appeared in his writings when he said:

> And to make plain to everyone the administration of this mystery, which for ages past was kept hidden in God, who created all things. His intent was that now, through the *ekklesia,* the manifold wisdom of God should be made known to the rulers and authorities in the heavenly realms, according to his eternal purpose that he accomplished in Christ Jesus our Lord, (Eph. 3:9-11).

Jesus Christ is the wisdom of God. Father wants the many facets of Wisdom (Jesus) to be expressed concretely through the body of Christ. What would the practical outworking of this look like? This is an endless subject, but at a minimum it would entail believers functioning together without regard for the divisions and barriers that are forces at work in the world—things like the poor/ those with more, male/ female, Jew/Gentile, employer/employee, and educated/uneducated.

Paul was gripped and driven by the purpose of God to see His Son come to expression on the earth through the *ekklesias*. We, too, should be captured by this vision of the eternal intention of God in Christ. Let your heart bask in this lavish revelation by reading Frank Viola's *From Eternity to Here*.

On the one hand, then, we have before us the glorious desire of God to have a Bride for His Son on earth. On the other hand, we have the obstacles and difficulties of incarnating the life of Christ together in community. Are we able to live "in Christ" with this undeniable tension in our midst?

Remember when the twelve spies were sent into the Promised Land? Ten came back afraid and ready to give up—"there are giants and huge challenges in that Land." Only two saw past what their eyes witnessed. The remnant with faith exclaimed, "The Lord will surely give us the Land." That Land was a shadow. Now the Lord gives us the Land, that is, Christ, both as individual parts of the body, and as a believing community. We would do well not to let the difficulties that lurk on every side keep us from pursuing Christ *together in our shared life.*

FIRST FRUITS

There is a reality about Christ that few are conscious of in their daily functioning. Jesus was the "first fruits" from the dead. His resurrection assures our bodily resurrection on the Last Day.

"First fruits" in Israel were dedicated to the Lord, and served as a "down payment," or "earnest," of the future full harvest. In other words, the "first fruits" were a present reality, but they pointed to a fullness that was yet to come.

This is how we have to view our life in Christ in this present evil age. Jesus is in us now, and Paul stated that we possess the "first fruits" of the Spirit. But our existence parallels the pathway of Christ. He first suffered and then by resurrection entered into glory. Likewise, Paul said, we suffer presently and groan for our glorification by resurrection. Thus, as Richard Longenecker noted, "the Christian life is ... expressed in a situation of temporal tension between what is already a fact, and what has yet to be realized," (*The Ministry & Message of Paul*, p. 101).

We live in the bright revelation of the Lord compared to those of faith living in the pre-resurrection era. Yet even though this is true, we still now "see through a glass darkly," and we do not yet know anything as we should, compared to the fullness of the harvest that will come.

We groan for the "face-to-face" at the glorious return of Christ. Right now, "it does not appear what we shall be; but we know that when He appears, we shall be like Him, for we will see Him as He is."

Realizing that we live in a time of "first fruits" will help us in several ways as we wrestle with the challenges of community life and God's glorious purpose for the *ekklesia* on earth. First off, knowing that we are functioning in a pre-harvest period will restrain us from utopian dreams about "the perfect *ekklesia*." Any expression of Christ on earth through His *ekklesias* on earth will be far from lily-white. Count on it!

Secondly, the "first fruits" perspective will encourage us to pursue the realities of Christ that have indeed broken into history. Christ is in us through the Spirit. Because of this, we actually do eat and drink of the heavenly gift and the Holy Spirit, hear the voice of the Shepherd, and experience the powers of the coming age. We should not view these realities in some minimalist fashion, but expect the "greater things" that Jesus mentioned.

So as we look to the Last Day, we must understand that it is not God's intention for us to "have it all" just yet. He has guaranteed that the "first fruits" will burst into a full-blown harvest of a New Heaven and New Earth, where such things as curse and tears will be no more, and we will feast on Christ as the Tree of Life forever. Having Christ now is gloriously real—but we cannot forget that whatever we experience in this life is still "first fruits"—a down payment for the harvest that we hope for—the hope for a "better resurrection."

In Romans 8, Paul pointed out that the whole creation is groaning for the "manifestation of the sons of God"; that believers groan for "the redemption of their bodies"; and that the Spirit supplicates for us with unutterable groanings. The creation awaits resurrection day when Christ's Bride will be resurrected, and the curse will be lifted from the earth. We await our manifestation and glorification when our mortal bodies are raised incorruptible and into immortality. The Spirit knows that everything is moving toward the simultaneous "glorious liberty of God's children," and the liberation of the earth from the bondage of corruption.

All of this "hope" in Christ should serve to spur us on "now" to be the communities (the Bethanies) where the fullness of His love in Christ may be displayed to the world's principalities, powers, and populations.

PART TWO: VOICES FROM THE BODY

"NEITHER BE CALLED 'LEADERS,' BECAUSE YOUR LEADER IS ONE, THE CHRIST."

CHAPTER 8

APOSTOLIC AUTHORITY: WHAT FORM DID IT TAKE?

Hans Van Campenhausen

> Many appeal to "apostolic authority" as a model for leadership in the church by pastors, etc. But what form did "apostolic authority" actually take in the early churches? Campenhausen decisively shows the various elements involved in their "authority."

On occasion Paul, who is constantly subjected to claims from every quarter (2 Cor. 11:28), declines to be burdened further with troubles and disappointments (Gal. 6:17); or again, he may threaten his refractory children with the spiritual 'rod,' (1 Cor. 4:21). He knows too what of love and respect is owed to his position as such (2 Cor. 2:3; 7:7; Phil. 3:20), and what, both inwardly and outwardly, he is entitled to by reason of his labors.

All this, as already pointed out, is really a matter of course, and in itself presents no particular problem. For the truly astounding feature of the situation we must look in quite the opposite direction, and consider the fact that Paul, who both as one called to be an apostle of Christ and as a teacher of his churches is a man of the very highest authority, *nevertheless does not develop this authority of his in the obvious and straightforward way by building up a sacral relationship of spiritual control and subordination.* Quite the contrary; whenever there seems to be the possibility of this, it is balked by Paul himself, who rejects in set terms either his right or desire to construct such an authority: 'Not that we lord it over your faith; we work with you for your joy, for you stand firm in your faith,' (2 Cor. 1:24).

Such expressions are not, of course, based on an appeal to freedom as an automatic human right, which Christians too possess within the Church; Paul is referring to the freedom of the Spirit, which belongs to the baptized children of God who have been liberated by Christ. This freedom is not only in conflict with any attempt to re-impose the old Jewish law; it is just as essential to maintain it whenever new, personal authorities arise within the congregation itself and seek to domineer over men's faith, or when Christians attach themselves to particular teachers and apostles, and quarrel over their individual qualities as if these were the things that mattered, (1 Cor. 3:5).

When the congregation came to the faith, they became subject not to their apostles and teachers of the moment, but directly to Christ himself.... Hence, it is these workers who belong to the congregation and not the other way around, (1 Cor. 3:21ff; 2 Cor. 4:5). To this rule even the apostolic 'founding father', Paul himself, is no exception. He is, it is true, the one who 'like a skilled master builder' laid the foundation, Christ, on which everything has to be built thereafter, (1 Cor. 3:10ff; Col. 2:6).... But this makes no difference to the freedom of the congregation: 'Was Paul crucified for you? Or were you baptized in the name of Paul?' (1 Cor. 1:13). *The apostle takes his place in the community for Christ, not before Him.*

This means that the power of command, which he exercises, is from the outset fundamentally limited. Paul has to guide his congregations; he sees the mistakes they are making, he is constantly aware how much they are still lacking in the spiritual maturity and 'perfectness' which ought to be theirs. But his position is not that of the prudent pedagogue, who will train his pupils up to freedom only a little at a time; *Christian freedom is already a fact at all times,* and must be recognized as such.... However imperiously Paul the apostle may demand a hearing for Christ, however ingeniously he may put himself forward as a pattern for imitation, yet he simply cannot give orders. He does not himself create the norm, which is then to be obeyed without further ado, but instead those who possess the Spirit must follow him in freedom; and it is this freedom which he has in mind when he addresses them. They must themselves recognize in his instructions the 'standard of teaching' to which they are committed, and to which Paul in a sense merely 'recalls' them, in order that they may affirm it for themselves, and freely and joyfully make it their own once more.

Paul, the apostle, knows what is at stake, and he knows in whose Name he admonishes 'by the grace given to him,' and has to speak. It is implicit for him in the fundamental confession of Jesus Christ that the ancient basic moral commandments are not open to discussion; within the church they must be observed. The real difficulty begins only when the instructions have to be given which go beyond these elementary principles into matters of detail, at the point where the sphere of relative decisions, of distinguishing between what is humanly good and better, begins.

The paradigm of such discussion is his treatment of the Corinthians' questions on the problem of marriage, (1 Cor. 6:12-7:40).... In giving advice Paul also bears in mind what is best for his people; but even so he may not 'lay any restraint upon them,' and must allow them their liberty in any matter that does not concern Christ and his word. Paul therefore deliberately refuses to interpret his authority in such a way that it could be extended beyond its proper sphere of upholding the truth of the Gospel to become a source of legal norms of any kind for the life of the Church.

But even when it is a question of the essential knowledge and preservation of the truth of the faith he avoids putting himself in a position of unqualified supremacy over his congregation. His 'children' are at the same time also and always his 'brethren'; and therefore he as an apostle is not their *'master'* but their servant for Jesus' sake.'

Paul is always producing new compound word-formations with sun ('co-') in order to bring out his fellowship with his congregations in their labors, their struggles, their prayers and consolations, their sufferings, rejoicings, and triumphs.... Even when revolted to the very depths of his soul by the horror of the alleged case of incest at Corinth and by the slackness of the congregation responsible for dealing with the situation, he has already delivered his judgment in advance and from a distance, he avoids presenting this decision, which seems to him the obvious one, as a unilateral measure taken solely by himself.

The congregation is to assemble, and, united with him 'in spirit' though separated in body, to carry out on the evildoer 'with the power of the Lord Jesus Christ what is in some sense the common judgment of them both.... By thus appealing to the congregation's own judgment and sense of responsibility he takes their freedom seriously, possibly indeed more seriously than they themselves had expected. Those who put the questions (to Paul) would probably have preferred to receive in reply a strict and binding decree. But it is precisely at this point that the distinctively Christian aspect of Paul's methods becomes clear; and this aspect can be misunderstood only by someone who has failed to grasp the very heart of Paul's purpose.

With this deference to the congregation, which is the vessel of the Spirit, goes a lively sense of what the distinctive character of his message requires in practice.... In fact his authority is of such a kind that he continually brings it to bear only with reserve, reluctantly, and, as it were, merely requesting or soliciting compliance, and confines its full and unambiguous exercise, in accordance with its essential nature, to such occasions as the true authority of Jesus himself determines. Precisely for this reason it is recognizable as the direct opposite of the false zeal of the Judaizing apostles, and of that dead, legalistic preaching, which has nothing more to offer than all too human requirements, commands, and prescriptions, (Col. 2:20).

The dispensation of the Spirit and of the new righteousness, of which Paul is the minister, possesses in its gentleness and moderation a different, more powerful and more resplendent glory than that of the old Mosaic law, with its letter that killed, because this dispensation is effected through candor, love, and patience, and the winning and reconciling power of forgiveness, and no longer through punishment and destruction, imposed by external authority....

There are, however, limits to this attitude, precisely because it is Christian in character. These limits are reached where Christ and his Gospel are themselves once more abandoned and betrayed, where genuine apostasy has begun. At this point Christ's apostle no more than Christ himself can pronounce anything but anathema and condemnation. In the event of conflict all that is necessary, so to speak, is for the apostle to lead them back to the ground which is their common starting-point in order that they and he together may in fellowship make from there the step which should and must be taken.

Paul's own conception of his authority, therefore, for all the intense emotion, and the directness which characterizes it, and the many levels at which it operates, is yet of monumental simplicity in that it is at all times organized entirely around one focal point, in relation to which everything else acquires its meaning: *Paul is the apostle of Jesus Christ*—he is this wholly and completely and nothing but this.... It is Christ, who out of sheer grace calls them to his grace, that the congregations become free and are to remain free. It is this that gives Paul's approach to his congregations its distinctive character. Unequivocal though it is, its dynamic is nevertheless at the same time genuinely dialectical, a combination of powerful thrust and gentle retreat, at once threatening and inviting.

It is understandable too that a later generation, even when it appealed specifically to Paul, should have failed to preserve his discovery. The later Church venerated its saints and 'good' apostles in retrospect without reserve, and saw them as possessors of an all embracing sacral authority, which should not be limited in any way. For them, therefore, the apostles became once more quite simply the 'foundation' of the Church.

Paul also differed from the later historians and dogmatic theologians of his Church in the fact that he attaches little importance to the neat definition of specifically apostolic authority in relation the authorities of other 'evangelists' and spiritual teachers. He constantly brackets himself with Barnabas, Apollos, and various other members of his congregation in a way that is highly significant. Such an attitude fits in well with his conception of the apostolate as entirely a matter of *proclamation*, not of *organization*. The Church lives by her awareness of the Christ-message, the Gospel; it is on this, and not on the privileged position of certain individuals whom God has called to his service for this purpose, that all depends. The emphasis on the special character and unique importance of the original apostolic office and testimony for its own sake is completely post-Pauline.

CHAPTER 9
THE RISE OF THE ONE-BISHOP-RULE IN THE EARLY CHURCH

Judy Schindler

INTRODUCTION

Even a cursory reading of the post-apostolic fathers reveals how faintly influenced they were by the doctrine, which had earlier, so consumed the apostle Paul's thought: *justification by faith.* This early literature reflects much more interest in matters of discipline, church polity and sacramental forms. In fact, as one modern historian puts it:

> The pre-Augustinian church never heartily accepted St. Paul's doctrine of justification by faith. Sometimes it was wholly ignored; at other times even when the formula was respected it was interpreted in a way which would have been expressed more naturally by saying that men are saved by repentance, (Reinhold Niebuhr, *The Nature and Destiny of Man,* 2 Vol. ed. [New York: Charles Scribner's Sons, 1941], p.132).

While the doctrine of justification by faith suffered at the hands of many different dogmas, the church's adoption of mono-episcopacy (one-bishop-rule) played a pivotal role in keeping this central doctrine always on the periphery of the church's attention. The hasty abandonment by the 2nd Century church of the N.T. form of plural oversight for its own form of one-bishop-rule is important for at least two reasons.

First, one-bishop-rule appeared in a church largely ignorant of the implications of justification by faith. The spiritual hierarchy resulting from the one-bishop-rule witnesses to the lack of comprehension of the spiritual equality possessed by all believers because of Christ's righteousness imputed to them.

Secondly, one-bishop-rule, once created, perpetuated itself at the expense of justification by faith. Any reformer who suggested that justification was a gift of grace threatened to undermine the established, hierarchical church structure. Grace, not hierarchy, was the historical loser in these conflicts.

Therefore, to understand the drift, if not stampede, away from the centrality of justification by faith by the pre-Augustinian church, it is also necessary to view the parallel rise of the one-bishop-rule. It is the intent of this article to examine some influential forces at work in the development and reinforcement of one-bishop-rule, and to briefly assess the fundamental significance of this rise. The writings of Ignatius of Antioch and of Cyprian of Carthage will be the primary sources used, as they adequately reflect the development during the period under consideration, (c. 100 – 250AD).

DEVELOPMENT OF ONE-BISHOP-RULE

The New Testament Model

The N.T. instruction regarding church leadership viewed an autonomous local body being cared for by plural oversight and the service of deacons. The group of elders in each local church was called a "presbytery," and there is no example in the N.T. of a church ruled by *one* elder, nor was there a "chief elder" exalted above the others. When occasion required a spokesman (Acts 15), he would be a representative and temporary one, not occupying a permanent office of supremacy.

The Ignatian Model

But by the beginning of the 2nd Century we find in Ignatius of Antioch having an almost complete disregard for the N.T. model, and a very well-defined replacement: one-bishop-rule. No longer are the terms "elder," "overseer" and "shepherd" used interchangeably (as one function viewed from different perspectives: elder empha-sizes maturity; bishop emphasizes *oversight* and *administration,* and shepherd empha-sizes *feeding* and *guarding.* Rather, the "bishop" is elevated above the "presbytery." What is more, the bishop was given supremacy. Ignatius wrote to the Magnesians, "be eager to do everything in God's harmony, with the bishop presiding in the place of God and the presbytery in the place of the council of the Apostles," (Robert M. Grant, ed., *The Apostolic Fathers: A New Translation and Commentary,* 6-Vols. [New York: Thomas Nelson and Sons, 1964], p. 58).

The bishop, according to Ignatius, is in the place of God and should be obeyed accordingly: "yield to him [bishop]—not to him but to the Father of Jesus Christ, to the bishop of all" (*Apostolic Fathers,* p. 58). And although the bishop, presbyters and deacons all receive respect and are not separated (*Apostolic Fathers,* p. 73), the duties given to the bishop leave no doubt as to the relative insignificance of the other ordained ministers. The bishop is to lead prayers in the church, celebrate the Eucharist and conduct baptismal meals, give counsel on matters of spiritual disci-pline and approve marriages, give homilies (sermons) and convoke councils of the church, (*Apostolic Fathers,* Vol. 1, p. 171).

Its Rapid Spread

By the middle of the 2nd Century the Ignatian model of one-bishop-rule had entered the West with Victor being described as a bishop of Rome. In the 3rd Century the

Apostolic Tradition of Hippolytus witnesses to an even more elaborated conception of the function of a bishop. He is the high priest, and as such has the duty to forgive sins by imposing penance and conveying absolution, (J .G. Davies, *The Early Christian Church: A History of Its First Five Centuries* [*Grand Rapids:* Baker Book House, 1965], p. 131). He also is responsible for overseeing the administration of the church finances and for ordaining other ministers, in addition to discharging the liturgical duties listed above.

The continual and deepening distinction between the bishop and his presbyters and deacons can be clearly seen in the following instruction regarding their ordination: When the deacon is ordained, there is no reason why the bishop alone shall lay his hands on him: he is not ordained to the priesthood but to serve the bishop ... but the presbyters shall lay on their hands because of the common and like spirit of the clergy. Yet the presbyter has only the power to receive; but he has no power to give, (The Apostolic Tradition of Hippolytus, trans. Burton S. Easton [Cambridge: Cambridge University Press, 1934; reprint ed., n.p. 1962], p. 38).

The Cyprian Model

Thus, by the time of Cyprian's rule as bishop of Carthage in the middle of the 3rd Century, the distinction of function has hardened into a separation and gradation of office: to move from one office to another is viewed as an advance or the result of the increased merit of the individual, (Davies, p. 133).

Cyprian's response to the inheritance of the one-bishop-rule form of church government was to strengthen it by developing the authority of the bishop. To support both concepts he defends the idea of an unbroken succession of bishops from Peter to the legitimate bishop in every Catholic Church. Furthermore, it is Cyprian who first formulates the unity of bishops into an organization, which represents the whole church:

> And this unity we ought firmly to hold and assert, especially those of us that are bishops who preside in the church, that we may also prove the episcopate itself to be one and undivided...the episcopate is one, each part of which is held by each one for the whole, (quoted by Earl D. Radmacher in *The Nature of the Church* [Portland: Western Baptist Press, 1972], p. 32).

Having traced the growth of one-bishop-rule as seen in Ignatius and Cyprian, let us now turn to a brief analysis of the factors, which may have stimulated this development.

INFLUENTIAL CULTURAL FACTORS

Synagogue Background

The most obvious influence on the early church's perception of how it should organize itself was Israel's synagogue-structure. The Jerusalem church was the greatest reflection of this influence, for it consisted mainly of converted Jews. As could be expected, there was some carry-over from synagogue worship into the new Israel's worship, (i.e., reading of the Scriptures, singing, exhortation, elders, etc; cf. Robert

Banks, *Paul's Idea of Community: The Early House Churches in Their Historical Setting* [Eerdmans, 1980], pp. 17-19).

It appears that in post-apostolic times James—who was apparently one of the "pillars" at the Jerusalem church (Gal. 2:9) —was exalted in an unhealthy manner. For example, the *Clementine Homilies* contain a letter from Clement to James: "Clement to James, the Lord, the bishop of bishops, who rules Jerusalem, the Holy Church of the Hebrews, and the churches everywhere excellently founded by the providence of God," (Richard Zehnle, *The Making of the Christian Church* [Notre Dame: Fides Publishers, 1969], p. 38). Eusebius tells us that James was the first one "elected to the throne of the Bishopric of the church in Jerusalem." It is unlikely that James exalted himself, but those who succeeded him evidently did. After his martyrdom, James' closest living relative (a cousin of the Lord), Symeon, was elected to his place, and the beginning of a dynastic principle is established, (Zehnle, p. 39).

Jewish Priesthood in the New Testament Times

The concept of the Jewish council made up of two elders and a president may certainly have influenced the Jerusalem church and subsequent churches. We know from post-apostolic writings that the Old Covenant idea of the priesthood was applied more and more exclusively to the one bishop as high priest, and very little stress given to the priesthood of all believers. This was amply witnessed to in the Apostolic Tradition and by Cyprian, (G.S.M. Walker, *The Churchmanship of St. Cyprian* [London: Lutterworth Press, 1968], p. 38).

Gentile Environment

1. *Associations:* The Gentile environment provided ample reinforcement for leadership by a graded hierarchy, which could lead to the abandonment of leadership by a plurality of equals. Edwin Hatch has drawn a picture of Roman society during the beginnings of the church in which associations played a tremendous role. There were associations of almost every kind: trade and dramatic guilds, burial and dining clubs, literary and financial societies. And these associations had much in common with the church (in organization): the same names for meetings and some of the same names for the officers, a common fund, common meal, open-admission (women, strangers, freedmen, slaves) (Hatch, *The Organization of the Early Christian Churches* [New York: Burt Franklin, 1972], pp. 30, 31). It would be easy for the church to adopt the associations' use of a "president" without much thought, for it was then a universal office, (Hatch, p. 84).

2. *Roman Government:* The Roman form of government also played its part in shaping the consciousness of the church. As early as 90AD, Clement of Rome compares the church to the army (Robert M. Grant, *Early Christianity and Society: Seven Studies* [San Francisco: Harper and Row, 1977], pp. 22, 23). And in the 3rd Century Cyprian takes Tertullian's application to the church of an embryonic form of constitutional

government and expands it. Cyprian's model for the church was the Roman Empire: just as its health depended on peace and unity which could only be protected by a universal obedience to its laws, so the church's health depended on peace and unity resulting from obedience to its laws. The provincial governors administered the Roman laws, the church's governors were its bishops, and "every act of the church is ruled by these very governors," (Robert F. Evans, *One and Holy: The Church in Latin and Patristic Thought* [London: Camelot Press, 1972], p. 48). The bishop in each place was a "judge in place of Christ." Like the provinces that had a council composed of delegates from the cities to discuss matters of common concern, so Cyprian's bishops gathered from cities to discuss matters in council, (Evans, p. 48).

INFLUENTIAL THEOLOGICAL FACTORS

Need for Church Unity

As great as the influences of the Jewish and Gentile environments were, they were eclipsed in importance by the pressures exerted on the young church by questions of doctrine and discipline. Both issues threatened to sunder the church. The remedy for both problems was sought in the establishment of a doctrine of church unity, the key to this unity being the authority of the bishop.

Ignatius: The Person of the Bishop

In his letters to the seven churches, Ignatius is primarily concerned with combating doctrinal error, since Judiazers as well as Docetists were stirring up the churches and threatening schism. The canon of N.T. Scripture had not been established, so Ignatius sets forth the person of the bishop as the measure of sound doctrine. He warns the Smyrnaeans against the Docetists: "All of you are to follow the bishop as Apostles ...Apart from the bishop no one is to do anything pertaining to the church," (Grant, *Ignatius*, p. 120). A Christian could be assured of his faithful obedience to God if he was obeying the bishop and preserving the unity of the local church. "For as many as belong to God and Jesus Christ, these are with the Bishop," (Grant, *Ignatius*, p. 99). Unlike Cyprian, Ignatius does not try to prove the authority of the bishops by succession (or through the Scriptures), but he merely posits it, with some reference to Christian tradition prior to himself, (Grant, "Introduction," p. 169).

By locating sound doctrine and right practice in the person of the bishop, Ignatius solved the problem of unity for a season. As we shall now see, the solution was not a final one, and needed a capstone to render it an impregnable defense.

Cyprian: The Office of Bishop

The next 150 years saw one-bishop-rule become secure in its acceptance by all the churches. And with the exception of some like Tertullian, no one is known to have challenged this form of government. The growing matter of concern, however, was "who is the rightful bishop?" An increasing competition by rival claimants to the bishop's office in the same city, or claims by schismatics to be the bishop, gave rise to the desire to identify criteria for judging these claims. Irenaeus seems to be the first to attempt to prove a succession of bishops from the Apostles, but it is Cyprian who undertakes the task of developing a coherent doctrine of church unity based on apostolic succession.

Apostolic Succession

In his treatise "On the Unity of the Catholic Church," Cyprian reasons from Matt. 16 that the care of the church was given first to Peter, the church being built on him. And, although the other Apostles subsequently received the same share of "Honor and Power," Peter was given the primacy so that "it may be shown that the Church is one and the See of Christ is one," (Anne Fremantle, ed., *A Treasury of Early Christianity* [Viking Press, 1953], p. 301). After establishing the basis of church unity on Peter's primacy, Cyprian takes a further important step in cementing the authority of the bishop over the church: he states that the Apostles themselves were the first bishops, (Evans, p. 49). Since the Apostles were given the judicial power of binding and loosing, forgiving and retaining of sins, and bishops were now being called upon to exercise this same kind of judicial power, certainly it must be seen that the Apostles then were the first bishops, (Evans, p. 49)! Therefore, to set oneself against a bishop was the same as refusing to obey the Apostles—and ultimately God Himself. So to those who disagreed with the Catholic Church, and withdrew to establish a different version of Christianity, he could write:

> And although the stubborn and proud multitudes of those unwilling to obey withdraw, yet the church does not withdraw from Christ, and the people united in their bishop and the flock clinging to their shepherd are the church. Whence you ought to know that the bishop is in the Church and the Church is in the bishop, and if there is anyone who is not with the bishop, he is not in the Church (*St. Cyprian: Letters,* trans. Rose B. Donna [Catholic University of America Press, 1964], Vol. 51, p. 229).

And to those who elected a rival bishop and declared their communion equally valid, Cyprian draws this line:

> Lawful bishops are made by a decree of God or divine ordination and since the church is one as God is, the appearance of a second bishop in the same See, setting up another church and dividing Christ's members, would contradict divine appointment, evangelical law and Catholic unity, (Walker, p. 42).

Unity of the Bishops

One other important link that Cyprian provides between Ignatius and a fully formulated doctrine of the ultimate authority of the bishop of Rome over all the church can be pointed out. For Ignatius, the bishop was seen as a local authority. However, Cyprian saw the bishops as an organization representative of the whole church in unity: "it is our duty to hold fast this unity that we may show that the episcopate itself also is one and indivisible," (Fremantle, p. 301).

And, although no bishop had supremacy over another since each received his power directly through the Apostles, the real autonomy of each bishop could not exist. Real autonomy for each bishop would create the possibility of serious dissent on doctrine or practice within the body of bishops, and the carefully sewn garment of church unity would be rent. So, Cyprian writes:

> In order that this unity should be manifested, it is essential for all bishops to be inspired and controlled by the same Holy Spirit; a bishop who breaks the concord of his brethren must at once be rejected from their fellowship ...it is obvious that he does not retain the Holy Spirit's truth with the remainder, (Walker, p. 43).

Despite Cyprian's inconsistency in applying this principle of concord among the bishops, the principle is well on its way to being applied in such a way as to smother not only destructive dissent, but also constructive dissent, as the bishops become the ultimate heads of the church, (cf. Chapter 3 of Leonard Verduin's, *The Anatomy of a Hybrid,* for an interesting treatment of this subject).

Resistance to Justification by Faith

Finally, a factor in the promotion of one-bishop-rule, which was suggested at the outset of this article, must be expanded. The early church's resistance to the gospel's claim that only the righteousness of God in Jesus Christ could vindicate guilty men before God's judgment took many forms, but the source remained the same: human arrogance looking for a way to vindicate itself, (Niebuhr, p. 127). The church after the Apostles had no clear perception of the problem of sin or its solution as found in the atonement. "The deeper problems of the Christian faith were partially obscured in some of the Apostolic Fathers and totally so in others," (Niebuhr, p. 130). Thus, generally speaking, in the post-apostolic church the authority of the bishop replaces the gospel of grace as the measure of truth.

The Need for One-Bishop-Rule

Indeed, the abandonment of justification by faith in Christ's righteousness created a vacuum that was ultimately filled by one-bishop-rule. First, since Christ's work for sinners was not understood to be the principle for interpreting the faith, there was a need for some trustworthy guide in the interpretation of Scripture to the people, namely, the bishop. Secondly, since man's efforts on his own behalf were so critical in his salvation, the need for temporal perfection was escalated. The defection and gross imperfection seen in many of those in the church, especially during persecution, undermined this ideal of perfection substantially, and caused the church to locate its identity in one man who could measure up in its eyes to the ideal of a holy man, namely, the bishop. Cyprian's formula, "the bishop is in the church and the church is in the bishop," encapsulates this idea. Evans points out that by this time "the eschatological purity of the whole church has become a sacral purity attached to her bishop," (*One and Holy,* p. 59).

The Results of One-Bishop-Rule

And finally, since the bishop was the interpreter of sound doctrine and the embodiment of moral perfection, it became imperative that this exalted and central position be defended from attack both from without and from within the church. Only absolute authority derived from the Apostles and held by the college of bishops of the Catholic Church could make secure the place of the bishop as the representative of the people before God. Thus, the result of the church's refusal to recognize the gospel of Christ's righteousness as primary was *one-bishop-rule,* and this in turn became the means by which the church was hindered in her recovery of this truth.

Concluding Remarks

Although many factors came into play in shaping the one-bishop-rule from 100 – 250AD, the lack of comprehension by the church concerning the significance of justification by faith created a situation where the door was opened for the fabrication of an authoritarian hierarchy. This hierarchy did fulfill the expectations of those who wanted conformity with the Judaistic and Roman heritage, and it did provide a kind of unity against divisive forces within and without the church. But the process, which resulted in the establishment of one-bishop-rule, swallowed up the priesthood of all believers. Further, in the centuries, which followed, one-bishop-rule was committed to silencing dissent and dissenters.

Finally, it is instructive to note that the momentum of one-bishop-rule was carried over even into the new reformation led by Luther, Calvin and Zwingli. While the gospel of justification by faith came to the fore, the affirmation of the priesthood of all believers was seen in the light of one's *individual* relationship to God through Christ, and not as a *corporate* responsibility to minister one to another. In actual practice, Protestants retained the one-bishop-rule in the form of one-pastor or one-minister rule. Some Anabaptists and their spiritual offspring saw more clearly the implications of the gospel in this area and sought to restore the plural ministry characterized in the New Testament. In our own day, much remains to be done in following their lead to restore mutual ministry in the body of Christ, and to intrude into the long-standing tradition of one-man-rule.

The post-apostolic "Bishop" came to rule over the church in certain geographical areas. The dominion of his rule was defined by some *territory* (i.e., Bishop of North Africa). The post-reformation one-minister-rule had more to do with how a local church was governed. Thus, while the territorial dimension of one-man-rule was in many cases abandoned, the one-bishop-rule in the local church still prevailed, and remains with us to this day. Even in many churches where there is a plurality of elders, the "Pastor" still retains functional precedence over the others. While the one-man-rule in the post-apostolic early church was expressed differently, the basic principle is the same as the one-pastor-rule that has reigned in post-reformation history.

For further reflection, see Elaine Pagels, *"'One God, One Bishop': The Politics of Monotheism," The Gnostic Gospels,* Vintage Nooks, 1979, pp. 28-47 & Jon Zens, "Body Life—Leadership" [audio], http://searchingtogether.org/audio-resources.html

CHAPTER 10

YOU ARE ALL BROTHERS & SISTERS: GROWING IN OUR UNDERSTANDING OF "AUTHORITY"

Bruce Davidson

JESUS & AUTHORITY IN THE GENTILE WORLD

To understand the nature of authority in the church we must first examine the teaching of Christ about this subject. Otherwise, we run the risk of misunderstanding texts relating to church life, because we might tend to interpret them against the background of the concept of authority that surrounds us.

When we look at the teaching of Jesus concerning authority among His disciples, we find two major points—He was opposed to:

1. Their imitation of the practice of authority in the Gentile world (Matt. 20:20-28; Mark 10:35-45; Luke 22:24-30)

2. The practice of religious authority in the Jewish world, (Matt. 23:1-12)

MATTHEW 20:20-28

In this passage, Jesus' remarks arise in connection with a dispute over who would sit at the right and left hand of Christ in the coming kingdom. It is striking to note how Jesus used this occasion of dispute as a springboard for some positive teaching. Many people argue that we should avoid controversial subjects like this because they can bring about disagreements among disciples. However, we should learn that moments of dispute could be used for our growth and the resolution of conflict.

Ironically, this passage comes just after Jesus predicts his impending death (vv. 17-19), His supreme act of self-giving. But the minds of the disciples are in another world—a world of power, status and prestige, where people are in competition with one another. Are we very different? We talk and sing about Jesus' humility, but at the same time our thoughts are often occupied with success, money, possessions, or our status as compared to other believers.

Jesus draws attention to the fundamental difference between the way things operate in the Gentile world, and the way they are to operate in His kingdom. Traditionally this passage has been taken as an explanation of what true spiritual greatness is—servanthood. But it also teaches us about the way authority is to come to expression in the church, and makes it clear that whatever authority might exist in the church, it is entirely different from the world's ideas about authority.

> Jesus called them together and said. "You know that the rulers of the Gentiles lord it over them, and their high officials exercise authority over them. Not so with you. Instead, whoever wants to become great among you must be your servant, and whoever wants to be first must be your slave—just as the Son of Man did not come to be served, but to serve, and to give His life as a ransom for many," (Matt. 20:25-28).

In verse 25 Jesus uses several words that describe the exercise of authority by Gentile rulers and proceeds to repudiate any application of them to relationships among His disciples—*"Not so with you."* The Greek word for "rulers" is archontes, which means "ones who are first," "ones who are pre-eminent."[1] It signifies someone who is "number one," the chief, the most important person, the one "in the spotlight," and is applied in the N.T. to governmental authorities (Acts 16:19; Titus 3:1), but *never* to church leaders. No one except Jesus Christ is "number one" in the church.

Other words Jesus uses are *katakurieuo* and *katexousiadzo,* which both have the prepositional prefix, kata, meaning "down upon" or "over." *Katakurieuo* means literally to "be a lord over"—gain dominion, subdue, master, or overpower.[2] In the Septuagint, the Greek translation of the Old Testament (O.T.), this verb is used in Numbers 32:22 where Israel subdued their enemies in battle. In Acts 19:16 an evil spirit *overpowers* or *masters* some Jewish exorcists, and beats them up. 1 Peter 5:3 uses this word to tell elders not to "lord it over" God's flock.

The other word, *katexousiadzo,* means to "exercise authority over," or sometimes possibly "tyrannize."[3] Both of these words do not necessarily imply any abuse of power, but only the exercise of a certain kind of power.

LUKE 22:25-26

This passage is similar to Matt. 20:20-28. The words used here are milder forms of the same word, minus the *kata* prefix—"The kings of the Gentiles lord it over them *(kurieuo),* and those who exercise authority *(exousiadzo)* over them are called Benefactors. But you are not to be like that...." Here, Jesus uses the simple word meaning to "exercise authority," *exousiadzo.* In other words, it is not simply a power-grabbing or tyrannical behavior that Jesus forbids in the church, but the very existence of this *exousia*-type authority is excluded.

Exousia, the usual Greek word for authority, has no evil connotations, as the word authoritarian does in English. It means "rightful, actual, and unimpeded power to act, or to possess, control, use, or dispose of something or somebody. While *dynamis* means simply physical power that is in some sense lawful."[4] Jesus exercised exousia when He cast out evil spirits, taught and forgave sins, (Mark 1:27; 2:9). 1 Corinthians 7:4 states that both husbands and wives have exousia over their spouse's body and hence conjugal privileges.

LUKE 7:1-8

This passage helps us to understand better the meaning of "authority." The centurion tells Jesus:

> I myself am a man under authority *[exousia]*, with soldiers under me. I tell this one, 'Go,' and he goes; and that one, 'Come,' and he comes. I say to this servant, 'Do this,' and he does it.

One of the key words here is "under." In *exousia*-authority relationships, there is a hierarchy of power, with everyone *under* somebody else, except the person at the top. In Rome it looked something like this:

1. Emperor

2. Provincial Governors

3. Lower Officials, Army Commanders

4. Centurions

5. Common soldiers, servants

Exousia-authority in this instance is

1. Hierarchical

2. Comes by virtue of an office one occupies

3. Cannot be opposed lawfully

Authority flows down from the top in a pyramid. On each level a person has the right to say to the ones below him," "*I* make the decisions; *you* carry them out." Even today this is the way most organizations function. In government, the President is at the top, under him is his cabinet, and under them are their respective bureaucracies. In the military, power flows down through the generals, colonels, etc., down to privates. In the business world, the president of the company or the chairman of the board has under him vice-presidents or managers in charge of various departments, and under them are more people. It is a very efficient and workable system, but it has some drawbacks. If the man above you is incompetent, disaster can result. Consider what happened in Japan—a land where hierarchy is very important:

> Sometimes respect for hierarchy gets dangerously out of hand. In 1981 Captain Seiji Katagiri of Japan Air Lines flew his DC-8 into Tokyo Bay, killing 24 of the 174 people on board. Investigations into the incident revealed that Katagiri was a borderline psychotic who probably crashed his plane intentionally. It was also discovered that his behavior on a previous flight had been so erratic and potentially dangerous that his co-pilot and flight engineer

58 To 0: How Christ Leads Through The One Anothers

had agreed to watch him closely and wrestle him away from his controls if necessary. However, they had not reported his behavior or spoken to him about it. As captain of the aircraft, Katagiri was a superior in the hierarchy whose authority was not to be taken lightly.[5]

Many people think the church is also a hierarchy that looks like this:

1. Christ

2. Bishops

3. Priests, Pastors, Elders

4. Congregational members

Maybe you think this reflects only a Roman Catholic or Episcopalian view of authority in the church. But just erase *bishops* and *priests,* and you have the typical view of many Protestant churches. Usually they see "the pastor" or "the elders" as fitting into a hierarchy of authority with Christ at the top and the congregation "under" him/them. But the trouble with this view is that it is a hierarchical *exousia*-authority, and Jesus said this kind of practice was unacceptable in His church: "not so with you."

The reason there can be no hierarchy in the church is that in the New Covenant, *all* Christians are priests and brethren, (1 Pet. 2:5; Matt. 23.8). There is equality of status before God, not hierarchy. The word *exousia* is applied to Christ the Head but is *never* applied in the N.T. to the role of elders. Other words are used which do not carry the same hierarchical force: *hegeomai,* "lead, guide" (Heb. 13:7, 17, 24); *proistami,* "direct, manage, administrate," (Rom. 12:8; 1 Tim. 3:4-5, 5:17); poimaino, "shepherd" (1 Pet. 5:2), and *episkopeo,* "care for, oversee" (1 Pet. 5:2).[6]

George Mallone states very well the implications of Matthew 20:20-28 for the eldership of a church:

> Contrary to what we would like to believe, elders, pastors, and deacons are not in a chain of command, a hierarchical pyramid, which puts them under Christ and over the church. The leaders of a biblical church are simply members of the body of Christ, not an elite oligarchy. They are members whom God has chosen to endow with certain *charisms.*[7]

NO HIERARCHY IN ACTS

In the book of Acts, we find that the apostles did in fact do what Jesus taught in Matthew 20:20-28—they refused to exercise hierarchical authority over the Jerusalem congregation. One writer summaries the testimony of Acts in this way:

> It is true that the apostles were clad with a very special authority in the early church, but it is also true that this in no way produced a hierarchical dictatorship. In the N.T. story, the decisions are taken regularly by the body of the congregation. When an apostle had to be chosen to replace the traitor Judas, it is Peter who moves the motion, but it is the congregation who puts forward the candidates, (Acts1:15-26). When men had to be chosen to see to the charitable work of the church, once again it is the Twelve who make the suggestion, but it is the congregation who do the choosing (Acts 6:1-6),

and the apostles who do the approving and setting apart. When Peter took the crucial step of admitting Cornelius the Gentile to the fellowship of the Church, it was to the congregation that he had to explain himself and to justify his action, (Acts 11:1-4). When the Council of Jerusalem took the great decision to open the doors to the Gentiles; the decision was approved by the apostles and the elders *with the whole church,* (Acts 15:22). When Paul called upon the Church at Corinth to take disciplinary action against the man guilty of notorious immorality, that action is to be taken "when you are assembled," at a meeting of the congregation, (1 Cor. 5:4). Leadership the apostles had, but in no sense did they have dictatorship. The decision was in the hands of the congregation.[8]

Jesus says that when we think of church relationships, *authority* is not the word and idea that should be in our minds and mouths. Two other words should be—servant and slave, (Matt. 20:26-27). A slave does not have much power, status, or authority. None at all, in fact.

OBJECTION:

What about Heb. 13:17, "Obey your leaders and submit to their authority" (NIV). Does this not imply that leaders are in a position of hierarchical authority?

First of all, the word *authority* is not in the Greek text, which says, "obey your guides and submit." Secondly, the exhortation to *submit* does not necessarily imply that hierarchical authority is in view. Sometimes instructions to submit in the N.T. have to do with hierarchical authority, (Rom. 13:1); sometimes they do not. In Ephesians 5:21 it is "submit to one another out of reverence for Christ." Every believer is to submit to every other believer, in the sense of accepting with humility that person's encouragement, help, or exhortation. No one would claim that everyone is over everyone else in the church. Paul also says in 1 Corinthians 16:15-16:

> You know that the household of Stephanas were the first converts in Achaia, and they have devoted themselves to the service of the saints. I urge you, brothers, to *submit* to such as these and to *everyone who joins in the work,* and labors in it.

Surely this everyone does not include elders only, since the whole household of Stephanas is in view, not only the men but presumably also women, and perhaps even servants and children.

I believe one problem Christians have had is that wherever they read the word submit in the N.T., they automatically think that *exousia*-authority is the object of the submission. This is a mistake. Hebrews 13:17 is best understood as an exhortation to "be persuaded by" the *teaching* of the elders, and submit to their *spiritual guidance,* not as a command to carry out the unilateral *decisions* of the eldership. Otherwise, it would contradict the spirit of Matthew 20:20-28.

We should avoid modeling our church relationships and activities after patterns taken from the world. In seminary, I once attended a "church management" seminar. It instructed future pastors on how to run their churches with an organizational flow-chart, like a corporation. This is also hierarchical behavior. Christians are always exhorting one another not to love the world and not to be conformed to the pattern of this present world, (Rom. 12:2). However, we rarely feel so concerned about how much like the world our church structures have become. If we are so zealous to maintain our spiritual separation from this present evil world in our individual lives, should we not be just as zealous not to pattern ourselves after this world in our church life?

OBJECTION:

If there isn't any hierarchical authority in the church, won't everything degenerate into chaos?

No, because the real Head, Christ, is present in our gatherings by the Holy Spirit to direct things, if we look to Him, (Matt. 18:20). *We are not a leaderless mob.* Perhaps one reason why authoritarian behavior keeps reappearing in church history is that we keep losing the conviction that Christ is present to lead and guide, so we rely on personalities and organization instead.

Do we really believe that Christ is present in the church as the Head of the church by the Holy Spirit working in each member? Do we really believe He has made a unified body out of the congregation, which will function harmoniously, if we pursue Him together? The very fact that we can ask such a question—won't it be chaos?—shows that we do not have much faith in the reality of the Holy Spirit implementing the Headship of Christ in our meetings.

JESUS & AUTHORITY IN THE JEWISH WORLD

Not only does Jesus teach His disciples not to imitate *exousia*-structures in the Gentile world, but in Matt. 23:1-12 He also teaches them not to copy the type of religious authority then current in the Jewish world. This authority came as a result of the exaltation of the Jewish teachers, the Rabbis.

> Then Jesus said to the crowds and to his disciples: "The teachers of the law and the Pharisees sit in Moses seat. So you must obey them and do everything they tell you. But do not do what they do, for they do not practice what they preach. They tie up heavy loads and put them on men's shoulders, but they themselves are not willing to lift a finger to move them. Everything they do is done for men to see: they make phylacteries wide and the tassels of their prayer shawls long; they love the place of honor at banquets and the most important seats in the synagogues; they love to be greeted in the marketplaces and to have men call them 'Rabbi.' But you are not to be called 'Rabbi,' for you have only one Master and you are all brothers. And do not call anyone on earth 'father,' for you have one Father, and he is in heaven. Nor are you to be called 'teacher,' for you have one Teacher, the Christ. The greatest among you will be your servant. For whoever exalts himself will be humbled, and whoever humbles himself will be exalted, (Matt. 23:1-12).

In 1st Century Judea, most scribes, the professional teachers of the law, belonged to the sect of the Pharisees, although not every Pharisee was a scribe. Held in high honor, the scribes had great influence and authority over their congregations and over Jewish life in general. This is till the case today among some Jews, such as the ultra-strict Hasidic Jews.

The Rabbis were preachers, and they preached in the synagogues. Of course, they usually did not say, "Thus says the Lord," but rather "Rabbi Akiva used to say...." They depended not so much on Scripture as on the traditions and writing of former Rabbis and commentators. Aside from this, their role in the congregations was similar in many respects to the role of the pastor in many churches today. They were the main preachers and teachers of the Word of God at that time.

The trouble is that the role of the teacher and the authority of God have been confused, both then and now. We tend to regard God's messengers with an awe that verges on worship *(latria)*. Auguste Sabbatier has written about this phenomenon:

> An innocent and natural delusion of popular faith in its first stages of devel-
> opment transfers the supernatural and divine character of the object to these
> organs by which the divine communicates itself or makes itself known. Thus
> among savage peoples the sorcerer is invested with magical potency.... Thus
> the words of the Catholic Priest for the peoples of his flock, and even those
> of the Protestant pastor for the ignorant among his people, become the very
> word of God.[9]

The Jews exalted the Rabbis in Jesus' time, and it is obvious that they enjoyed their special status. They paraded their piety in every conceivable way. The most important seats in the synagogue were the ones of the elders and teachers, which were the farthest in front and faced the congregation.[10]

Even outside the synagogue, their special status was recognized in the greet-
ings they received and titles they were given. Rabbi comes from the Hebrew word *rav*, meaning "great" or "chief," so that rabbi means "my great one."[11] The Rabbis even like to be called "father" and claimed a right to greater honor than a man's parents, since parents gave only physical life, whereas the Rabbis gave spiritual life by their teaching.[12]

In Matthew 23: 8-12, Jesus teaches against any such thing among His disciples. He forbids them to be called or to call any person in the church by titles such as "Rabbi," "father," or "teacher." Robert Gundry appropriately calls this passage "The Prohibition of Honorific Titles in the Church."[13]

Nowhere in the N.T. are any Christians called by titles such as these.

Everyone is called simply by name or else "brother/sister so-and-so."

Even the apostles are not referred to by using titles; such as, "the apostle Paul arrived in Corinth." In Acts, Luke calls him simply "Paul" (Acts 14:1; 16:3), and Peter refers to him as "brother Paul," (2 Pet. 3:15).

I have observed that the use of titles such as "Pastor" or "Preacher" do indeed go hand in hand with the exaltation of teachers. Once I ate with a family that con-
stantly referred to their pastor as "Pastor," as in "Pastor was sick yesterday." Another person wrote me once, that "Preacher will be gone this weekend." The exalted role of these men was so great that their title even swallowed up their names!

Probably many people envy Prince Charles because he is heir to the throne of England. But the Christian is a child and heir of the King of the universe. Why should he want to be exalted any more than that, or to see anyone else in the church exalted any more? Martin Lloyd-Jones said in his book Preaching & Preachers:

> To me the work of preaching is the highest and greatest and the most glorious calling to which anyone can ever be called.[14]

I respect Martin Lloyd-Jones greatly, but I must take exception to this statement. Just being a child of God and disciple of the Lord Jesus Christ is "the most glorious calling to which anyone can ever be called." In the N.T. you do not find people glorying in what an exalted thing it is to be a preacher.

CONCLUSION:

The real glory and authority in the church belong to God the Father and our Lord Jesus Christ. But by elevating teachers and preachers like the Jews of Jesus' day, and by setting up *exousia*-type hierarchies like the Gentiles, we have obscured that sovereign glory in the life of our churches.

Jesus makes it clear: "the greatest among you will be your servant." Rather than modeling our church relationships after the unbelieving world around us, we should follow the teaching and example of our Lord.

Notes:

1. W. Arndt & F Gingrich, *A Greek-English Lexicon of the N.T.* (University of Chicago, 1975), p. 113

2 *Ibid.,* p. 413

3 *Ibid.,* p. 422

4. J.D. Douglas, ed., *The New Bible Dictionary* (Eerdmans, 1962). pp. 111-112

5. Jared Taylor, *Shadows of the Rising Sun* (New York: William Morrow Co., 1983), p. 47

6. Arndt & Gingrich, pp. 344, 690, 713-714, 299

7. George Mallone, *Furnace of Renewal* (IVP, 1981) p. 85

8. William Barclay, *By What Authority?* (Judson Press, 1975) p. 116

9. Auguste Sabbatier, *Religions of Authority and the Religion of the Spirit* (McClure, Phillips and Co., 1905), pp. 279-280

10. William Barclay, *The Gospel of Matthew,* II (Westminster Press, 1957), p. 317

11. J.D Douglas, *The New Bible Dictionary,* p. 1072

12. Barclay, *Matthew,* II, p. 317

13. Robert Gundry, *Matthew: A Commentary on His Literary & Theological Art* (Eerdmans, 1982), p. 453

14. D. Martin Lloyd-Jones, *Preaching & Preachers,* p. 9

Bruce Davidson is a professor at Hokusei Gakuen University in Japan. He is the author of "A Contrite Heart is Better than an Esteemed Self: How Self-Esteem Ideology Contradicts Reason and the Bible," *Hokusei Review, The School of Humanities,* 44:1, September, 2006, pp. 55-72, and "The Four Faces of Self-Love in the Theology of Jonathan Edwards," *Journal of the Evangelical Theological Society,* 51:1, March, 2008, pp. 87-100.

CHAPTER 11
CHURCH LEADERS & THE USE OF HONORIFIC TITLES

Darryl M. Erkel

> "But you, are you seeking great things for yourself?
> Do not seek them." (Jeremiah 45:5)

The Lord Jesus, in His condemnation of the Pharisees recorded in Matthew 23, plainly forbids His followers from either giving or receiving honorific titles. Whereas the religious hypocrites love "respectful greetings in the market places, and being called by men Rabbi" (v. 7), this is not to be the mark of Christ's disciples: "But do not be called Rabbi; for One is your Teacher, and you are all brothers. And do not call anyone on earth your father; for One is your Father, He who is in heaven. And do not be called leaders; for One is your Leader, that is, Christ. But the greatest among you shall be your servant. And whoever exalts himself shall be humbled; and whoever humbles himself shall be exalted" (vv. 8-12).

Jesus is neither denying functional differences within the church, nor is He suggesting that it is wrong to call one's biological parent "father." Rather, He is prohibiting the use of self-exalting and honorific titles of distinction among those who have chosen to follow Christ. While conferring honorific titles upon prominent religious authorities may be the way of the world, it is not the path that Christ has called us to pursue.

Yet, in spite of the clarity of Jesus' command, Christians have historically ignored His words. We continue, for example, to address our church leaders as "Reverend," "Doctor," "Minister," or "Pastor," and, unfortunately, far too many of them are glad to receive such flattery and even love to have it so! Commenting on the words of our Lord in Matthew 23, the noted N.T. scholar, R.T. France, has perceptively written:

These verses, while still commenting on the practice of the scribes and Pharisees, are addressed directly to Jesus' disciples, warning them against adopting this status-seeking attitude. "Rabbi" (v.8) and "Master" (v.10) probably act here as synonyms. They are titles appropriate only to the One Teacher (v.8), the Christ (v.10), in relation to whom all His followers stand on an equal footing as "brethren".... Over against that unique authority His disciples must avoid the use of honorific titles for one another ("Christian rabbinism," Bonnard)—an exhortation which today's church could profitably taken more seriously, not only in relation to formal ecclesiastical titles ("Most Rev.," "my Lord Bishop," etc.), but more significantly in its excessive deference to academic qualifications or to authoritative status in the churches, (*Tyndale New Testament Commentaries: Matthew* [Leicester, England: Inter-Varsity Press, 1985] p. 325).

Church history, according to J.C. Ryle, has all too clearly demonstrated that we have missed the true meaning of Jesus' words:

Happy would it have been for the Church of Christ, if this passage had been more deeply pondered, and the spirit of it more implicitly obeyed. The Pharisees are not the only people who have imposed austerities on others, and affected a sanctity of apparel, and loved the praise of man. The annals of church history show that only too many Christians have walked closely in their steps, (*Expository Thoughts on the Gospels*, Vol. 1 [Grand Rapids: Baker Book House Reprint, 1977] p. 299).

Greg Ogden, a writer and church leader, states:

I mourn for the church because we seem to display so many of the characteristics that Jesus said, "Not so among you" (Mark 10:43). Shameful arrogance and haughtiness have reached epidemic proportions among church leaders... A direct implication of Jesus' servant stance was His obliteration of titles... We have refused to take Jesus' words at face value. Jesus' obvious intent was to remove any basis for "lording it over" others by dispensing with titles that give people an elevated place in the "pecking order." We all occupy the same level ground at the foot of the one Teacher, Jesus Christ. We are not "great ones" or "lords"... Finally, do not accept the designation "master" or "leader." No human can usurp the position of the head of the body, Christ. Our tendency seems always toward idolatry, to make someone larger than life. Never forget: Jesus alone is Lord, (*The New Reformation: Returning the Ministry to the People of God* [Grand Rapids: Zondervan, 1990], pp. 172, 174).

It is important to emphasize that such terms such as "elders," "overseers," and "pastors" are functional terms, and were never intended to serve as formal titles. In other words, the terminology is descriptive of one's task; they help to picture someone's function, or may even denote one's spiritual maturity as in the term "elder." Thus, it is just as foolish and unnecessary to speak of "Pastor Bob" as it is to speak of one who possesses the gift or function of hospitality as "Hospitality Harry"; or one who has the gift of mercy as "Mercy Mary"; or one who has the gift of giving as "Giving George."

While seeing nothing inherently wrong with titles *per se,* even Craig L. Blomberg, associate professor of New Testament at Denver Seminary, is compelled to recognize its dangers:

> But one wonders how often these titles are used without implying unbiblical ideas about a greater worth or value of the individuals to whom they are assigned. One similarly wonders for how long the recipients of such forms of address can resist an unbiblical pride from all the plaudits. It is probably best to abolish most uses of such titles and look for equalizing terms that show that we are all related as family to one Heavenly Father (God) and one teacher (Christ)... In American Christian circles perhaps the best goal is to strive for the intimacy that simply makes addressing one another on a first-name basis natural, (*The New American Commentary: Matthew,* Vol. 22 [Nashville, TN: Broadman Press, 1992] p. 343).

If we were to look at education only, we might conclude that the apostles of our Lord were not particularly trustworthy, since none of them (except Paul) had any recognizable formal training: "Now as they observed the confidence of Peter and John, and understood that they were uneducated and untrained men, they were marveling, and began to recognize them as having been with Jesus," (Acts 4:13). Moreover, "teachers amongst the Lord's people do not need titles granted by men as a sign of theological authority to teach; authority and ability to teach in spiritual things come from the Lord through the Holy Spirit, and not through the schools of men. Such titles, both then and now, distract from the pre-eminence of Christ over all those who are brethren in the family of God... We are all brethren and we are all servants *(diakonos)*; this excludes self-exaltation. God reverses what man would esteem," (J. Heading, *Ritchie New Testament Commentaries: Matthew* [Scotland: John Ritchie, LTD., 1984] pp. 307-308).

Greg Ogden writes:

> We get the kind of leaders we deserve. It often seems that the world's view of greatness is the standard we use when we select our leaders. We have allowed arrogant, unaccountable, and self-professed channels of the Spirit to shoot off like loose cannon. We sometimes have a penchant in the Christian community for holding up the proud and arrogant as our ideal because "they get the job done." Using the world's view of power, we want leaders to exercise influence, work their way into positions of power, and throw their weight around. We therefore get what we ourselves honor— Christian leaders who act like potentates rather than self-sacrificing servants of Jesus Christ. Our actions show that we do not believe that real power is expressed through servanthood that leads to a cross. The Church Growth Movement has identified strong pastoral leadership as a key ingredient in the growth of a congregation. I will grant that leaders must lead. But what gets passed off as leadership often has no resemblance to servant leadership as modeled and taught by our Lord... Our natural tendency is to concentrate power at the top, but Jesus modeled and taught a different way of life (*The New Reformation,* pp. 172-173).

Honorific titles help to perpetuate the "clergy-laity" division. While it is common for people to speak of church leaders as the "clergy" and the rest of God's people as the "laity," the N.T. never divides the body of Christ into two classes known as "clergy" and "laity."

The root meaning of *kleros*, from which we get our word "clergy," is "inheritance" or "lot" and refers to the believer's inheritance in Christ, not to a special class of ministers. The word laos, from which we get our word "laity," refers to all of a group; in some cases, it specifically denotes the people of God. Thus, all believers in Christ are part of the laos (or "laity"). Every believer is a minister and priest before God with authority to do the work of ministry, (1 Cor. 14:26; Eph. 4:11-16; 1 Pet. 2:5,9; Rev. 1:6). The N.T. never confines "ministry" to a select few.

> It is critically important for Christians today to understand that the language we use to describe our church leaders has the power to accurately reflect biblical thinking and practice or, conversely, to lead us far away from the true Church of Jesus Christ and into the false church. Words such as clergyman, layman, reverend, minister, priest, bishop, ordained, and ministerial convey ideas contrary to what Jesus Christ and His apostles taught. Such terminology misrepresents the true nature of apostolic Christianity and makes it difficult, if not impossible, to recapture it. As a result, most of our churches are in desperate need of language reform, (Alexander Strauch, *Biblical Eldership*, pp. 32-34).

CHAPTER 12

WHO'S IN CHARGE? QUESTIONING OUR COMMON ASSUMPTIONS ABOUT SPIRITUAL AUTHORITY

Matthew and Christa McKirland

INTRODUCTION AND THESIS

Who has authority and who does not? This question drives many debates in the church today, and the conclusions drawn from it determine how people can function. But very rarely do we ask the question, *what is authority?*

We propose a reframing of authority that defines how we function as a Christ-centered community. Being a Christ-centered community should be our primary concern, and from this pursuit our understanding of authority should arise. This article seeks to re-examine new-covenant believer (NCB) interpersonal authority, questioning the appropriateness of individuals exercising authority over fellow disciples of Jesus.[1] We contend that we must primarily emphasize how to mature as members of Christ's communal body and how to exhort others toward maturity, so that we, as a Christ-centered community, might fully express who Jesus is to the world.

COMMUNITY IS PRIMARY

Central among the thematic elements of Scripture is the notion of community. Many point to the themes of kingdom and covenant as the most pervasive ideas of the Bible, but community may be even more fundamental than these, as both kingdom and covenant found themselves on community. All things were created by a triune, communal God who cast his image onto humanity, and community is an integral part of who we are as humans. But, what is community? Considering the whole of Scripture, we define Christ-centered community as *a group of diverse, but equal individuals, interdependent on one another and united in love by the pursuit of a shared, transcendent purpose.* We contend that community, thus, consists of six foundational characteristics: shared transcendent purpose, unity, diversity, equality, love, and interdependence. While there is overlap, none of these distinctives can be actualized independently of the others.

EQUALITY

Within this diverse body, united by the Spirit of God and called to the purpose of modeling Christ in community, is a powerful realization of equality, demonstrated primarily through the use of family language. The significance of the family in the ancient Greco-Roman world is far different than that of our modern, Western understanding. While we might think of the husband and wife bond as the closest relationship in our society, in ancient Mediterranean society, the "tightest unit of loyalty and affection is the descent group of brothers and sisters."[2] It is fitting, therefore, that the sibling model becomes the chief and defining relationship between members of the body of Christ.[3]

Matthew 23 highlights the centrality of familial language to the new-covenant community.[4] Jesus contrasts the behavior of the religious leaders of his day with the way his followers are supposed to live humbly with a mindset of equality, saying,

> But you are not to be called "Rabbi," for you have only one Master and you are all brothers/sisters. And do not call anyone on earth "father," for you have one Father, and he is in heaven. Nor are you to be called "teacher," for you have one Teacher, the Christ. The greatest among you will be your servant. For whoever exalts himself will be humbled, and whoever humbles himself will be exalted, (Matt. 23:8-12).

On the basis of the brother-sister relational model, no one person should exalt himself or herself above others. God is Master and Father, and Christ is Teacher. Essential authority is in God, and the intimacy of the sibling relationship is to govern the New Covenant believer's interpersonal relationships in Christ-centered community. This strong sense of equality founds itself on the humble love modeled by Jesus, (Phil. 2:5-11).

Further, the concept of partnership in the gospel is significant, as we see brothers and sisters laboring alongside one another in the advancement of the gospel. We see this primarily in the letters of Paul as he uses honorable titles to refer to men and women in various communities, not to bring them glory, but to glorify the God of the gospel. Phoebe is a leader, "patron [or great help] of many" (Rom. 16:2);[5] Priscilla and Aquila are "fellow workers in Christ Jesus" (Rom. 16:3); the church at Philippi consists of those who have entered into "partnership" with Paul (Phil. 1:5), "partakers" (Phil. 1:7), and two women among them who are in conflict are even called those "who have labored side by side" with Paul, (4:2-3). In many other places, Paul commends those who contribute to the mission of the gospel, but never calls anyone his "disciples."[6] Paul knew that being a member of Christ's body meant serving with others since "the life of freedom involves interdependence, particularly with those who belong to the Christian community, resulting in a mutual serving of one another."[7] On the basis of mutual service within community we find a proper lens for viewing authority.

A REORIENTATION OF OUR VIEW OF AUTHORITY

Given this understanding of community and authority, we suggest that, rather than viewing community through the lens of authority, we should view authority through the lens of community. In Luke 10, when the 72 return after being sent out by Jesus with authority over the spiritual realm, Jesus says to them:

> Behold, I have given you authority to tread on serpents and scorpions, and over all the power of the enemy, and nothing shall hurt you. Nevertheless, do not rejoice in this, that the spirits are subject to you, but rejoice that your names are written in heaven, (Luke 10:19-20).

Clear authority is given to Jesus' disciples over all the power of the enemy and over all spirits, yet Jesus calls his followers to rejoice not in their authority, but in their inclusion among the communal people of God. The identity markers of Christ's community do not include badges of authority, even over evil, but those of being God's children (Rom. 8:14-17) and heirs of the promise, (Gal. 3:29).[8] While followers of Christ clearly have authority over the spiritual realm, interpersonal authority does not seem to make the list of vitals to body life.

An emphasis on the command authority of one or even a few over a Christ-centered community sets a dangerous precedent. It strips dignity from the community comprised of believer-priests who are conduits for the authority of the Spirit of God in union with the word of God. This emphasis also shifts the focus from the Chief Shepherd to a person(s). Today, if leaders are striving for or strongly advocating command authority in their communities, then they communicate a message that members of the community are incapable of living out their priesthood apart from a human authority figure to manage them. Too often, the preservation of order or the final say in a decision is used as an excuse for prominent authority structures in churches. Yet, what messages do such structures communicate to the body as a whole? Do they prompt others to maturity? Do they allow for the outworking of the authority of his Spirit? Do they encourage the use of spiritual gifts?

A heavy emphasis on the authority of individuals also takes away from the involvement of the community in decisions that guide and direct the group. In the New Testament, most of the letters are written to the entire community, and thus frequently use the plural "you" when they come to community life. Even in matters of church discipline, responsibility rests in those immediately involved and then proceeds to include the community at large, if necessary, for the sake of restoration, (Matt. 18:15-20; 2 Cor. 13:1; 1 Tim. 5:19). The level of dignity of each person in Christ-centered community is great, and leaders, as mature followers of Christ within the community, serve to guide and assist others out of their own gifting as they grow from immaturity to maturity in their relationships with Jesus.[9]

A DE-PROFESSIONALIZATION OF MINISTRY

Too often, educational institutions train women and men to build ministry around their own particular strengths or giftedness, and thus primarily edify the one being trained and not the body as a whole. Those who construct ministry around their personal giftings fail to uphold the message of Ephesians 4:11-13. Unfortunately, students at such educational institutions become doctrinally knowledgeable, but often may be left spiritually immature, not receiving adequate spiritual formation avenues or given practical training in building up the body of Christ. This results in overdependence on an individual:

> Remove the pastor and most Protestant churches would be thrown into a panic. Remove the pastor, and Protestantism, as we know it would die. The pastor is the dominating focal point, mainstay, and centerpiece of the contemporary church. He is the embodiment of Protestant Christianity.[10]

The pastor is the life of many churches. Quite unfortunately, many churches suffer and/or die when that pastor moves on or fails due to the pressure of fulfilling more than what's reasonable for one member of the body to fulfill. The body theology we find in Romans and 1 Corinthians leaves no room for a one-person show. "Paul rejects the idea of certain people in the community possessing formal rights and powers over ordinary members."[11] This would seem to speak to the language of "office" and the title of "senior" pastor among Christian communities as a human construction meant to elevate individuals beyond what the Scriptures state.[12]

You might be wondering how we could have diverged so far from what the Spirit intended when he inspired the human authors to pen our Scriptures. According to research done by William David Spencer, this divergence can be traced to the publication of the *Didache* in the 2nd Century.[13] This church discipline manual curtailed Christian freedom significantly, as a method for baptism was instituted, rituals were required, and the exercise of spiritual gifts was discouraged. Women were restricted from serving and, eventually, this led to restrictions on men being allowed to serve as well, thus creating the second-class "laity." This document was introduced to limit abuses that were happening within the church, but ended up creating more abuses than it corrected.

How do we start turning back the clock on eighteen hundred years of misdirection? A helpful starting point is the de-professionalization of ministry, specifically the pastorate, through modification of our language and rhetoric: eliminating titles such as *senior* pastor and labels such as *clergy* and *laity*. When one person is elevated above the rest, it is difficult to motivate individuals to pursue their gifts, and be satisfied with their value to one another and to God. The concept of leadership as an office to be filled by the pastor contributes to viewing ministry as a specialized endeavor only for an elite few.[14]

There is often a huge bifurcation between clergy (pastors, evangelists, teachers, etc.) and laity (everyone else) that communicates active value to the former and passive unworthiness to the latter.[15] The whole of the N.T. does not affirm this distinction, but instead affirms a single, unified body with unique functions of mutual service and empowered ministry based on gifting. Calling, gift, and maturity are inextricably linked to fulfilling the purpose of the body, and our structures need to encourage these.

CONCLUSION:

This article calls into question how we have defined NCB interpersonal authority and argues for reorientation through the lens of Christ-centered community. With the overarching question of the gender debate centering around the authority women can and cannot have in relation to men, we would do well to begin by asking: what authority can any NCB have over any other NCB? When we refocus on how the community of Christ can be most built up so that all members are pursuing maturity in Christ, the issue of interpersonal authority seems far less of a concern and ultimately unnecessary. Perhaps, after having highlighted the harm of an unbalanced view of authority, which leads to an over-professionalization of ministry and an under-mobilization of the body of Christ, more emphasis can be placed on the practical steps of equipping the entire body to utilize its gifts.[16] In this way, we focus more on Christ so that individual believers can discern the authority of the Spirit within them in the context of community. With this priority in mind, the mature can help the immature grow to look more like Christ, not through their assumed positional authority, or "office," but by serving one another in true community.

Notes:

1. This article only seeks to discuss the role of spiritual authority. Secular authority structures (government, business, education, etc.) not founded on the authority of God are not our concern here. These authority structures do not require the indwelling of the Living God and, as such, are governed by different principles and take on a different texture than Christ-centered community. Christ-centered community is meant to be supernaturally governed and stand in contrast to secular authority structures, (Rom. 13:1-7, Mark 10:41-44).

2. Joseph H. Hellerman, *The Ancient Church as Family* (Minneapolis, MN: Fortress, 2001), p. 36

3 *Ibid.,* p. 35

4. While the new-covenant community is uniquely defined by its equality (Gal 3:28), this is a new development in comparison with the old covenant. There were clear disparities in terms of race, class, and gender under the old covenant. However, under the new covenant, anyone can be a part of God's family, and not just any member of the family, but a privileged "son," (Rom 8:14). A sign of this new covenant is now baptism, and not the exclusive practice of circumcision. The priesthood is no longer of the Levitical order, but all are now part of the kingdom of priests. Hence, the equality characteristic of new-covenant community supersedes the inequality of the old order.

5. a. properly, *a woman set over others,* b. *a female guardian, protectress,* patroness, caring for the affairs of others and aiding them with her resources (A.V. Succourer): Rom. 16:2. Joseph H. Thayer, *Thayer's Greek-English Lexicon of the New Testament: Coded with Strong's Concordance Numbers* (Peabody, MA: Hendrickson, 1996), 549.

6. This disciple language is used one time in Acts 9:25, but it most likely refers to Paul's disciples from when he was a Jewish rabbi before he encountered Christ. We would do well to model this practice by not calling anyone our "disciples" but use language that emphasizes our coming alongside other brothers and sisters as we are discipled by Jesus together.

7. Robert Banks, *Paul's Idea of Community,* p. 181

8. While not within the scope of this article, one insight that has emerged is that we often overestimate the authority we have over other human beings, but underestimate the authority we have over spiritual beings.

9. In the passages that describe the function of these leaders, authority language is not present; leading and guiding language is (1 Tim 5; 1 Pet. 3).

10. Frank Viola and George Barna, *Pagan Christianity? Exploring the Roots of Our Church Practices,* Revised and Updated (Carol Stream, IL: Tyndale, 2008), p. 106

11. Robert Banks, *Paul's Idea of Community,* p. 132

12. This is seen when people ask: "Do you think women should be ordained?" Such a question emphasizes the position of the person. If we shift the question to "Do you think women are Spirit-gifted to have any of the spiritual gifts?" then we may ask, "How are women able and encouraged to serve in their Spirit-gifting within the body?"

13. For his complete article, see William David Spencer, "The Chaining of the Church," at ChristianityToday.com, 1988, http://www.christianitytoday.com/ch/1988/issue17/1725.html (accessed 2012).

14. The Greek terms translated as *office* in English occur very rarely in the New Testament, and on all but two occasions they are used to describe priesthood in the Old Covenant. The two occasions where *office* is used for ministry-related purposes (Acts 1:20 and 1 Tim 3:1) make use of an abstract form of the noun, allowing for office to be implied. Ralph Earle, "1 Timothy," in *The Expositor's Bible Commentary,* ed. Frank E. Gaebelein, vol. 11 (Grand Rapids, MI: Zondervan, 1978), 363. The terms *ierateia* (Luke 1:9; Heb. 7:5) and *episkopē* (1 Pet 2:12; Luke 19:44; Acts 1:20; 1 Tim. 3:1) connote the word office. Forms of *episkopē* are employed in Acts 1:20 and 1 Tim 3:1 in relation to ministry. Acts 1:20 quotes Ps 109:8 ("may another take his office!") and refers to the replacement of Judas among the twelve Apostles; 1 Tim 3:1 speaks of overseers and proceeds to list qualifications (the vast majority of which are without contest related to character) for such people. The term *episkopos* (translated "overseer") occurs five times in the

N.T. and does not necessarily imply office. Though office may be implied with these Greek terms, we believe that gifting should determine the function of overseers and elders in the body of Christ (along with all other functions), in addition to biblical qualifications found in 1 Timothy 3.

15. We would urge everyone to eliminate "laity" from one's vocabulary. As Marshall states, "I. firmly believe that many of our problems regarding ministry generally would be mitigated by a less rigid understanding of ordination and by getting rid of the unbiblical distinction between clergy and laity." I Howard Marshall, "Women in Ministry: A Further Look at 1 Timothy 2," in *Women, Ministry and the Gospel: Exploring New Paradigms,* ed. Mark Husbands and Timothy Larsen (Downers Grove, IL: Intervarsity, 2007), p. 54

16. Adapted from material discussed by Walt Russell, Ph.D. This illustration shows the difficulty of this paradigm shift.

Article adapted from original. First published in *Priscilla Papers,* Vol. 27, Issue 1 (Winter, 2013): 15-25. Used with permission of the authors.

Matthew and Christa are both pursuing MA degrees in Bible Exposition at Talbot School of Theology in La Mirada, California. They co-authored "Born to Lead: Born to Equip" in CBE's *Mutuality Magazine* (Summer 2009), and served together at Mosaic Whittier in California for the past five years. They hope to speak and write more on this topic in the future.

"The increasing size of the congregations, as they grew from being compact house-assemblies into looser aggregations of people less intimately bound to each other; the growing need for organization and order, and the resulting emergence to power of the men of affairs in place of the men of the Spirit... Prophets were now relegated to a lower place...The Bishop, on the other hand, steadily advanced in prestige and power, and became the leading figure in worship. Bousset maintains that it was the control of worship that was the first rung of the ladder on which he mounted to his pre-eminence in the Church."

—**Alexander B. Macdonald**, *Christian Worship in the Primitive Church*, T & T Clark, 1934, pp. 70-71

CHAPTER 13
NEW TESTAMENT PEOPLE ARE RESPONSIBLE PEOPLE

A verbatim transcript of a message on 1 Corinthians 7 by Hendrik Hart

I Corinthians 7 is an exciting and puzzling chapter. It is a portion of the Word of God; yet it contains several passages in which the author disclaims that his message is from God. I would like to discover with you that these passages are in a glorious way God's Word to us.

Chapter 7 begins with "Now, concerning the matters about which you wrote." The Corinthians, as all N.T. Christians, are aware of the fact that in the N.T. dispensation there is much less precise ruling about specific dimensions of life than in the O.T. Christians are in many ways on their own. Well, not quite their own, because, as the prophet Joel had foretold and as had been fulfilled at Pentecost, the Spirit of God had been poured out on all flesh. That means in the N.T. era we are confronted with the restoration of the people of God in their own responsibility. In the O.T. only some kings and other leaders had the Spirit of God. In the N.T. it is on all flesh. And that is what we have to take a hold of.

In verse 25 Paul recommends this unusual chapter by saying that he gives his opinion as one who by the Lord's mercy is trustworthy. Why can Paul be trusted? His ground for that comes in verse 40: "I think that I have the Spirit of God." But that instantly makes 1 Corinthians 7 a difficult chapter for us to be in touch with what one may call the deeper things of life.

We are not so terribly sensitive to the underlying spiritual currents of our age. We live on the surface. And so it is hard for us to come to terms with 1 Corinthians 7 because it depends not only on Paul's being certain that he has the Spirit of God, but also on whether or not we dare to walk confidently because God's Spirit is upon us.

UNUSUAL ADVICE

Let's go back to the first verse—"Concerning the matters about which you wrote." Paul is now going to give some advice to the Corinthians regarding the difficulties with which they have confronted him. And Paul does not do what one might have expected of a leader of God's people. Even though the people are confused he does not precisely tell them what they should and should not do. But he deals with them as responsible people. Listen to what happens in the first sixteen verses, where Paul gives much advice, but every time he gives advice he leaves room for the people to find the appropriate response to God's calling:

- Verse 1 – it is well for a man; verse 2 – but....
- Verse 5 – do not refuse one another except perhaps....
- Verse 7 – I wish that all were, but each has....
- Verse 8 – it is well for them; verse 9 – but if....
- Verse 10 – I give charge; verse 11 – but....
- Verse 12 – to the rest I say; verse 15 – but....

That's unusual isn't it?

In fact, he does more things in this chapter that are unusual, because when he talks about 'I recommend this, but....' he does not show those two elements over against one another as: this is the right thing to do and the other is not right. He characteristically in this chapter, as for example in verse 38, says that "he who marries his betrothed does well, and he who refrains from marriage does better."

We are accustomed to regard what Paul holds out before us as the right thing to do, and if you do something else you do wrong. Paul says you might do one thing, that's all right, and you might do another thing, that's even better. An unusual approach.

Paul, is, as it were, with the aid of the Spirit, working through priorities in doing good. It is very important for us to remember that Paul presupposes in 1 Corinthians 7 that he is speaking to God's people, who have God's Spirit. He assumes that he is speaking to a people who are spending their lives struggling with Gods' will, being puzzled by the difficulties of the age in which they live, knowing that some people have to go this way in life and other have to do different things, and how do you judge that? All that is presupposed.

But then Paul has priorities. Verse 7: "I wish that all were as I myself am, but each has his own special gift from God." What a kind way to proceed. He is not saying, that man does things differently from what I do, he must be wrong, but seeing these things as God's gifts. Then he says there are priorities. Some things are pretty good, other things are even better. And the gifts about which he is talking are not the gifts of chapter 12, the talents, so to speak. The gifts that Paul is talking about here are gifts in terms of walking in God's way in certain difficult circumstances. You remember how Christ talks about the eunuch that way; he takes a difficult road that is not given to all. That is the kind of gift Paul means. And in each dispensation we all have different gifts of grace.

MAKING UP OUR OWN MIND

And now comes the real difficult part of 1 Corinthians 7. Paul dares by the Spirit of God to say things about how God's people must go that must have seemed to Bible believing Corinthians, folk who knew the O.T. very odd. The chapter concentrates mostly on marriage, but the significance of it goes much deeper than that, as can be gleaned from verses 17 to 24, which for a moment take leave of the specific problem of marriage and tells us that the apostle is really placing the matter in a larger context. The marriage chapter is only an occasion for him to teach God's people much deeper things of wider significance.

What does Paul do? In verse 12 comes that first time "to the rest, I say, not the Lord." And in verse 25 – "now concerning the unmarried, I have no commandment from the Lord but I give my opinion as one who is trustworthy." Then verse 40 – "in my judgment she is happier if she remains as she is. And I think I have the Spirit of God."

If you found these things in 1 Corinthians 7 without any further reference, that would be strange enough. But we must also look at these pieces of advice, in their even stranger context. Paul is as it were talking about things here that go directly against the whole consciousness that God had been careful to develop in the people of the O.T. and deals with matters with which Christ had specifically dealt when he walked among his people.

What Paul does in this chapter is to relativize marriage. It is one of the things for which some are gifted and others are not. He says that not to be married is a more excellent way. Now you must remember Genesis. Marriage is not something that once upon a time some people decided to institute amongst themselves as a neat way of doing things. It is God's way with his people. "Therefore shall a man...." Well, says Paul, in this day and age, the way I perceive things, not the Lord but I, you understand.... It's not merely that he dares to listen to what the Spirit has to say to the churches. He dares to accept what the Spirit says even if it seems very odd in the context of what the Scriptures so plainly teach.

Or look at that section between verses 12 and 16 where Paul says that when a believer and an unbeliever are married. As could so easily happen in a missionary situation, one partner may have been called out by God and the other partner remains an unbeliever; and that leads to trouble. In such a meeting of faith and unbelief, then it might be better to separate. That too is a hard word to say. If you get the testimonial of the meaning of marriage—faithfulness until death do us part—then, Paul says, in that situation he sees room for separation.

But then 1 Corinthians 7, which is in the New Testament, is a typical example of how God sets his people before him in their restored responsibility. If they have been given the Spirit, then let them act in that way, in the teachings that Comforter works in their hearts. It's much more comfortable to have some leader tell us what to do. It is much more comfortable to have a synod decide that this is what we may do and that is what we may not do, than to find that the Word of God ask us that we be responsible. Paul says this is my advice, but I understand the complexities of your life; you make up your own mind. Not arbitrarily. You don't as it were decide in yourself. But you know God, you know his Word, and you know his Spirit, don't you? And together this difficult process is engaged in. Still, that is a scary business for an unspiritual generation as we are. So how do we solve the problem?

FOUR BIBLICAL GUIDELINES

In pouring over this chapter we can find at least four important indications which the apostle gives that become guidelines for deciding the difficult questions of life. Life is full of events for which the Scriptures do not have chapter and verse. How does a Christian then decide weighty issues?

One guideline:

The first guideline that Paul gives is found in verse 14 – "The unbelieving husband is consecrated through his wife and the unbelieving wife is consecrated through her husband." For Paul, that is an argument in part of his advice, where he wants these people to stay together. That is his first choice. The believer and unbeliever should stay together. Paul digs back into the O.T. and he hauls out and displays before the congregation the covenant. The covenant is very much a counting on the ordinary ways in which people relate to one another and influence one another. And once again it is clear that the apostle counts on the fact that he is writing to people who love God and who struggle to find out his will. So stay together. Be a salting salt. No light under a bushel. The power of the gospel works into the environment in which God's people testify to their new life. So that's one rule that Paul gives. If you are facing a difficult decision, in what way does your decision help you in penetrating into your environment with the great goods of God's salvation?

Second guideline:

Then, in verse 17 through 24 he advises the Corinthians to witness to their environment without being revolutionary about it. The gospel is dynamite. You don't, as it were, have to add your own to it. Where the gospel is obeyed, where the people live out the Word, it penetrates with great power into the environment. That's why Paul's advice in verses 17 through 24 is, if you have a difficult decision to make, you stay where you are, no matter what your job is, no matter where you were when you were called, there you witness, there you live as God's child. But there again Paul understands that in the context of his general rule, of not prescribing to the people, showing them the room they have in which to act. Verse 20 – "Everyone should remain in the state into which he was called. Were you a slave, asks Paul, never mind, but.... It does not become an iron rule in season and out of season, for if you can gain your freedom avail yourself of the opportunity. Become a mature Christian. Do not become a slave of the circumstances, but in God's name rule over the world in which you live redemptively. Use the opportunities that come your way in the service of the coming kingdom of God.

Third guideline:

The third policy that Paul follows in this difficult chapter is that we must be able to read the signs of the times. We must understand that God's creation is a historical creation, that things happen, that there is a movement forward to the coming again of Jesus Christ. And in that movement all kinds of things change and we must be in the Spirit to be aware of what has changed and why and how we should react to it.

So where does Paul get the courage to say, if you can possibly manage it you had better not marry these days, going seemingly against Genesis? Well, he says, I think that in view of the impending distress it is well for a person to remain as he is. Once again when Paul speaks this way he is not laying down a rule for the churches from time immemorial until the Lord comes again. But he shows us that we must be sensitive to the times in which we live.

God teaches us to seek the perspective of God's kingdom, the gospel is full of that: "Seek ye first...," and out of that relativize whatever comes your way, be it good or be it bad. Verse 29 – "The appointed time is short. From now on let those who have wives live as though they had none." Or verse 31 – "those who deal with this world as though they had no dealings with it...." Be engaged with this world from a certain distance. It is not wrong to be sad but don't drown in it. It's not wrong to be happy, but don't forget everything else in the world. Look at it from the perspective of the coming kingdom—this is only a way in which the kingdom comes. The kingdom is where it's at. So that in my life's affairs I can be sensitive to the times and decide what is and what is not important.

Fourth guideline

There is one more general strategy that seems to play a role in 1 Corinthians 7. Paul gives interesting advice, which we must not fail to understand the way it is intended. It comes down to this, when finally in doubt, let peace and tranquility prevail.

God calls a man to leave his father and mother and to become one flesh with his wife, to show God's order, God's shalom in the goodness and greatness of the institution of marriage. But, says Paul, if you are married to an unbeliever and that leads to nothing but strife, when your apparent obedience becomes nothing but an anti-symbol of the gospel, because it is ultimately a collision of the kingdom of God and the kingdom of darkness, when that is the case, it's time to get out because God must rule as a God of a new order.

And the same thing we find in verses 32 to 35: "I want you to be free from anxieties." That has to be read carefully. The unmarried man is anxious about pleasing the Lord, that's all right; the married man is anxious about worldly affairs, how to please his wife, and his interests are divided.

That's not right away to be condemned. Remember, it's all right to be married; it's better not to be married. But says Paul, when you are trying to make a decision in this, think through how it is going to contribute to your being a child of God.

When we think that Paul wants us to see this as a general rule for much wider application, how is that going to help us serve God? What Paul is saying is that when it comes to major choices in life (marrying is a major choice, seeking a job is a major choice, or moving to another city, these are the kinds of things for which psychologists give a lot of anxiety points; that's because people feel in their bone and marrow that these are decisions that have far reaching consequences). Should we not enter into those on our knees struggling with God. "Is this move really going to help me serve You better?

CALL TO RESPONSIBILITY

Now, that was a scary business, wasn't it, that we must be responsible people. But don't you think these guidelines help? How do I penetrate into the environment with the gospel? How can I change things without being a revolutionary? How can I make something of the times in which I live and do justice to the historical period in which I am born? And finally, how does it contribute to my serving God with joy and gladness? That's not that hard is it? I mean, it's possible, especially if we should be able to do it with God's Spirit, on our knees, having his Word as close as this to us and being in the fellowship of believers that can strengthen us in making these choices.

1 Corinthians 7 is a real N.T. chapter. It not only calls us to our responsibilities, but it also does so in a comforting way. God knows his people; He does not ask too much of them.

This article used with permission. It originally appeared in *Searching Together*, 12:2, Summer, 1983.

CHAPTER 14
THE REDEMPTIVE MODEL AND THE HOLY SPIRIT'S WORK IN THE EKKLESIA

Russ Ross

OVERVIEW

1. Introduction
2. Strengthening the Primary Link
3. The Eschatological Age of the Spirit
4. The "Testing" Motif: The Holy Spirit's Work in *Dokimazein*
5. The Mediating Factor: The Law of Christ
6. Conclusion

I readily admit that this study is far from final or exhaustive. It is, however, my prayer that some of the issues that I have focused on will be useful and instrumental in the initiation of constructive interaction, re-visiting some vital issues, and opening up new vistas of our life in Christ.

I acknowledge my full indebtedness to Jon Zens' article, "As I Have Loved You" [1] as focusing upon the correct and necessary starting point for Christian ethics in general, and as forming the nucleus and organic foundation for suggesting a new chapter in the "ethics of salvation history" in particular.

STRENGTHENING THE PRIMARY LINK

In order to strengthen our primary link, "as I have loved you," it is necessary to reiterate some of what Jon Zens has said. I am in full agreement with the thesis of "as I have loved you," namely:

This supreme act of love on the cross becomes the reference point, the starting point and the touchstone of all Christian obedience.[2]

For the sake of theological precision, it may be necessary to comment on the words, "This supreme act of love on the cross," because in the historical setting of John 13-17 the cross had not yet occurred! This is in no way to deny that the cross is in view (John 15:12-13). It most definitely is, as the later "Pauline" pattern indicates. It is, however, a significant fact that John 13:34-35 is *pre*-crucifixion. This places more emphasis *on the totality of the perfect humility and life of the unselfish, self-sacrificing giving* that Christ exemplified in His earthly life and ministry. In other words, Jesus had already, at that time, provided a "redemptive" example. He had demonstrated an unparalleled love to His disciples and the multitudes. The commandment was "new" *(kainos)*[3] in a refreshing and *qualitative* way, precisely because He had set the standard, and the disciples thus had a concrete *present* example to imitate.

One way to strengthen the "primary" link is to point out the general sphere of the Christian *walk*. Speaking in general categories, the Christian's entire *walk* is patterned after the redemptive-event/moral-demand motif. This is most clearly seen in Ephesians 5 where the believer's "walk" in mentioned several times (vv. 2, 8, 15), while the redemptive model is set forth in verse 2: "And walk in love, *as Christ also has loved us,* and has given Himself for us an offering and a sacrifice to God for a sweet-smelling savor." The reason I have pointed out these verses, which deal with the general nature of the Christian walk, is that they provide the unifying, all-encompassing platform from which everything else flows.

Another way the "as I have loved you" motif is strengthened by observing that set in the midst of the foot-washing episode and the "new commandment" is the announcement of Christ that after His physical departure, *the Spirit will come.* The imminent death of Christ becomes the occasion for both the announcement of the *ethic* and its *dynamic.* It is not surprising, therefore, that the most basic fruit of the Spirit is *"love"*—a love rooted in the new exodus, (Gal. 5:22; Rom. 5:5).

It is the sphere of the work of the Spirit in general, and in "testing" *(dokimazein)* in particular, that we now turn to in order to forge the next link.

THE ESCHATOLOGICAL AGE OF THE SPIRIT

The Holy Spirit's "role" in N.T. ethics cannot be over-emphasized. As Geerhardus Vos has well observed:

The impotence of sinful human nature for good, one of the Apostle's profoundest convictions, would likewise postulate the operation of the Holy Spirit along the whole range of ethical movement and activity. The marvelous efflorescence of a new ethical life among the early Christians in its contrast with pagan immorality, and its impulsiveness and spontaneity as compared with Jewish formalism, would of themselves point to a miraculous, supernatural source, which could be none other than the Spirit of God. Still further, the fact that to Paul the Spirit is preeminently the Spirit of Christ and therefore *as thoroughly equable and ethical in His activity as the mind of Jesus Himself,* will have to be remembered here.[4]

Furthermore, it is not too much to conclude:

> The manifestation of the power of the Spirit in the church is a fact that has no parallel and no direct antecedents in the Old Testament.[5]

In qualitative contradistinction from the old age, the inherent "betterness" and "newness" of the new age was:

> That through the Spirit of Christ the church was brought into existence, and that ever since in an uninterrupted flow the Spirit is operative in believers as an edifying power, (1 Cor. 14:1-19). That is to say, what had been an intermittent manifestation in the O.T. and seemed to be an equally temporary manifestation in Jesus, which now became continuous. Whereas in the old covenant the manifestation of the Spirit was limited to outstanding personalities, now it became characteristic of the average person in the church.[6]

This distinguishing "marvelous efflorescence," as Vos put it, in the work of the Holy Spirit is what Oscar Cullman realized to be the "key" to "all N.T. ethics." The inner working of the Spirit in the life of the regenerated believer was one of the decisive, marked features which was prophesied for the new age (Jer. 31:33-34; Ezek. 36:26-27). It is this train of thought that "the Spirit is again and again the gift of the great time of redemption, the content of the ancient promise of redemption."[7]

The eschatological gift of the Holy Spirit in this new age can even be seen as the liberating "deliverer" in a New Exodus motif. Hence in Galatians 5:18, "if you are led by the Spirit, you are not under the law":

> Which at once recalls the leading of Israel by the pillar of cloud and the pillar of fire (Exod. 13:21-22)—symbols of God's presence and guidance, which are also the essential functions of the Holy Spirit; thus in Galatians Paul thinks of the Spirit as effecting an Exodus out from under the confinement of the law.[8]

Being *in the Spirit* is a life of "liberty" and "freedom" from detailed law codes. And it is precisely by means of the *Spirit's working in and through* the consciousness of the renewed believer that he is able to walk in Christ's life.

It is the proper emphasis on the *Spirit's work in the believer* at this point in redemptive history that Oscar Cullmann found to be the "key to all New Testament ethics."

> The working of the Holy Spirit shows itself chiefly in the "testing," *dokimazein,* that is in the capacity of forming the correct Christian ethical judgment at each given moment, and specifically of forming it in connection with the knowledge of the redemptive process, in which, indeed, the Holy Spirit is a decisive figure.[9]

This Spirit-driven dimension of salvation history did not form in a complete vacuum, just as the "starting point" did not either. In the upper room discourse, Jesus had spoken of the Spirit, and of His future promised work and indwelling of the disciples, (*cf.* John 14:16-17, 26; 15:26; 16:13-15).

THE "TESTING" WORK OF THE HOLY SPIRIT

Definition – To begin with, the Greek word *dokimazein* can be translated **A.** "to test, examine, prove, scrutinize, (to see whether a thing be genuine or not), as in metals; **B.** to recognize as genuine after examination, to approve, deem worthy."[10] Hence, the primary[11] sense of "testing," "proving," "scrutinizing," as it contextually acquires its secondary meaning of "approve" or "recognize," progresses into a key concept when it is brought into relation with the will of God.

ROMANS 12:2

This is borne out by the Apostle Paul in Rom.12:2, one of the major exhortatory sections, which encompasses the whole spectrum[12] of ethical life: "And be not conformed to this age; but be transformed by the renewing of your mind, *that you may prove* what is that good and acceptable, and perfect will of God." It is significant that Paul here *assumes* and *presupposes* the believer's redemptive-historical status "in Christ," and then founds and anchors his exhortation (imperatives) on the whole schema of redemption (chapters 1-11, indicative). It is the Christian's "reasonable service" (12:1) to be "a living sacrifice" to God, and he "owes" it to God, as it were, because of what He has done.

It is specifically in the "renewing of the mind" *(nous)*—the building up of the image of God in humans by the Holy Spirit—that impetus is provided for being able to "perceive," "recognize," and "approve" the will of God. In this context, the *dokimazein* is *approving* and not so much "to prove" as the King James has it.

> It is approve.... But it is this meaning with a distinct shade of thought, namely, to discover, to find out or learn by experience what the will of God is, and therefore to learn how approved the will of God is.[13]

This "approving" of the will of God relates specifically to our *reciprocal relationships* with our Christian brothers and sisters and *mutual edification* by means of spiritual gifts (12:3-8). Then it goes on to have implications for our social and governmental relationships.

This N.T. strain regarding spiritual "testing" and "approving," of using and exercising mature reason and judgment, is again a key factor of life in Christ. It is in line with and accentuates the diversity and discontinuity of the old and new ages.[14]

> Hence, whereas in the old covenant the individual was to "determine the things which are best instructed out of the law," in the new covenant the Christian is to "test all things" and determine the things, which are "best" by reference to the working of the Holy Spirit in his life.[15]

In the process of spiritual maturation the believer will develop and progressively sharpen his reasoning faculties by means of *experientially* determining what is ethically best in a given situation.

THE MEDIATING FACTOR: THE LAW OF CHRIST

The primary way that this "testing/proving" motif becomes a practical reality in the believer's life is through the "law of Christ" *applied*, (Gal. 6:2). In order to avoid being charged with "antinomianism" and "mysticism," it is necessary to maintain that although the old covenant external law code, as a covenantally binding ethical standard has been "husked" away (Col. 2:14-15; Eph. 2:15; 2 Cor. 3; Heb. 8:13; etc.) from the new covenant believer, this is not tantamount to meaning "without law" *(anomos)*. The new covenant believer is not left to transient, existential whims, but is "in-lawed" *(ennomos)* to Christ (1 Cor. 9:21).

The law of Christ is a standard that is in itself opposed to rigid and forced legalism.

> Undoubtedly the expression "law of Christ" (Gal. 6:2) is meant to contrast with the system of legalism as a religious principle. It involves submission to a person rather than to a code.... All that Christ has become to the believer incurs a new kind of obligation upon him. As Christ bore the burdens of others, so the believer must do the same. This is the "law" of true Christian relationships.[16]

Thus the law of Christ is specifically realized in practice by the bearing of one another's burdens. This necessitates reciprocity and the integrating of the various members of the body of Christ. It requires intimate fellowship and keen sensitivity to our fellow brethren, alongside a real willingness to be servants of each other. The *means* whereby this is accomplished is through the inward personal working of the Holy Spirit.

The "law of Christ" is the "new commandment" to *love*. And *love* is the supreme fruit of the Spirit. Thus it is the interrelation and interaction of Christ's "law" with the Spirit's work that makes up the "spiritual-ethical" complexion of the believer:

> Without the mind of Christ through the activity of the Spirit at work in the believer, the principles of the law of Christ remain remote and unattainable.[17]

The "law of Christ" redemptive model, and the Spirit's work of *dokimazein* ("testing") unite to provide a healthy atmosphere of "Christian liberty" in ethics (Gal. 5:1,13).

CONCLUSION:

In conclusion, then, I hope that it has become apparent how "ethics in salvation history" has been extended. Beginning with the "as I have loved you" redemptive-model, I have tried to show a necessary connection, not only of the Holy Spirit's work in the new covenant believer in general, but also His work in aiding and determining our ethical decisions in particular.

This "testing" and "approving" motif of the Spirit's work takes on concrete expression through the "law of Christ," (Gal. 6:2; 1 Cor. 9:21), as well as through the multifarious dimensions that flow from the redemptive model. It is my prayer that this study will be challenging end edifying in our endeavor to walk worthy of the calling by which we are called.

Notes:

1. Jon Zens, "As I Have Loved You: The Starting Point Of Christian Obedience." BRR, 1X:2, p. 5

2 *Ibid.,* p. 5

3. "Suppose there is a machine for turning out lead pencils. The millionth lead pencil is new in the neos sense, although it is precisely the same as the 999,999th that went before. On the other hand, *kainos* means new in quality, new in *character, unfamiliar,* fresh, introducing something which has not been there before." William Barclay, *Unity and Diversity in New Testament Theology,* Eerdmans, 1978, p. 74

4. Geerhardus Vos, *Redemptive History and Biblical Interpretation,* Pres. & Ref., n.d., p. 122

5. Otto A Piper, "The Novelty of the Gospel," *Saved by Hope,* ed. James I. Cook, Eerdmans, 1978, p. 148

6 *Ibid.,* pp. 148-149

7. Ridderbos, *Paul: An Outline of His Theology,* p. 233

8. Eldon J. Epp, "Paul's Diverse Imageries of the Human Situation and His Unifying Theme of Freedom," *Unity and Diversity in New Testament Theology,* ed. Robert A Guelich, Eerdmans, 1978, p. 109

9. Oscar Cullman, *Christ and Time,* Westminster Press, 1950, p. 228

10. Joseph H. Thayer, *Thayer's Greek-English Lexicon of the N.T.,* Zondervan, 1962, p. 154

11. "*Dokimazo* is not uncommon in its primary sense of 'testing': along with other various nuances in the early papyri manuscripts, hence: 'his excellency the *epistrategus* shall sift the matter with the utmost equity.' It is used in connection with 'discernment,' 'in order that you may judge of his present condition': and in reference to one who examines calves, 'an inspector of calves for sacrifice.' From 'proving' to 'approving' was a step taken long before these documents were written, so that the ambiguity which meets us in Romans 2:18 and Philippians 1:10 is based on the normally coexisting uses. So in the earliest known marriage contract...differences between husband and wife are to be settled by three men, 'whom both *shall approve.*' The word is also used in reference to physicians who have 'passed the examination" (J.H. Moulton and G. Milligan, *The Vocabulary of the Greek New Testament,* Eerdmans, 1930, p.160).

12. "It will be observed how comprehensively he (Paul) surveys the whole range of human action and conduct. He starts from the consideration of people as constituting 'many members in one body,' and he proceeds to direct them in their various functions. He passes in review the private and public duties to which they

might be called—ministering, teaching, exhorting, giving, ruling, and obeying; he depicts the Spirit of the Christian in business and in rest, in joy and in sorrow, in hope and in tribulation, towards friends and towards enemies, in peace and in wrath. And he lays down the Christian principles of civil government and civil disobedience. It is a picture of life in its length and breadth, and even in all its lights and shadows, transfigured, as the landscape by the sun under the renovating influence of those spiritual rays of love which illuminated and warmed the Apostle's soul" (Wace, *Christianity and Morality,* p.147; cited by E.H. Gifford, Romans, James Family, 1977, p. 204).

13. John Murray, *NIC Commentary on the New Testament – Romans,* Vol. 2, Eerdmans, 1968, p. 115

14. "Each person in every situation 'must ever-examine anew what the will of God may be.' To this end, 'intelligence, discernment, attentive observation of the facts' all come into live operation, and the actual alternatives and the possible consequences are clearly and carefully assessed. Only after this kind of consideration may a decision be made in confidence and freedom" (James T Laney, "An Examination of Bonhoeffer's Ethical Contextualism," *A Bonhoeffer Legacy,* ed. A.J. Klassen, Eerdmans, 1981, p. 302).

15. Richard Longenecker, *Paul, Apostle of Liberty,* Baker Books, 1964, p. 195

16. Donald Guthrie, *The New Century Bible Commentary – Galatians,* Eerdmans, 1975, p. 286

17. Richard Longenecker, *Paul, Apostle of Liberty,* Baker Books, 1964, p. 194

This article originally appeared in *Searching Together,* 11:2, Summer, 1982.

"Perhaps nowhere is [this creative energy] more impressive that when we observe the young churches as they yielded themselves up in their worship-assemblies to the control of the Spirit of God, and, trusting to it wholly, adventured out on uncharted seas of spiritual experience, where they discover, once and for all, that in Christ they have encountered the very power of God Himself, and in a form adaptable to every sphere of their living."

—**Alexander B. Macdonald**, *Christian Worship in the Primitive Church,*
T & T Clark, 1934, p. 5

CHAPTER 15

THE CHURCH—A DISCERNING COMMUNITY

J. Lawrence Burkholder

We are living in an era of change and the call for change is now being directed to the church. The church has traditionally been a conservative institution. One of the roots of its conservatism is probably that it has always somehow claimed to have special connection with Deity, and Deity is sometimes thought to have resided outside of history in a rather static state, like the platonic conception of God, which has influenced Christian theology.

THE CHURCH IN THE WORLD

But today we are coming more and more to realize that the church is in history and if the church is going to be relevant in this world it must regard itself as a historical institution, even though it is, and quite properly should be, regarded as the body of Christ and as having a special relationship with God.

In fact, we have come to think of God as being active in history rather than apart from history. If you read the O.T., you will find that God establishes nations and kingships, and guides historical events. God is involved in history. The church must be that community which tries to understand what is going on in the world.

Now this call for change in the church is everywhere these days and many people are trying to think out patterns for renewal in the church. A number of experiments are going on, especially in the urban communities. People are trying new patterns in worship and, more importantly, in the arena of mission. The question is: How can we really contact the world and witness to the world and be properly influenced by the world?

DISCERNMENT

One of the questions that has been going through my mind for some time is the question of how the church may know the will of God in relationship to the world today. I don't know how you could ask a harder question, a more profound question, yet a question, which is most intimately related to what the church must be about. My thinking has been stimulated by what I find in the New Testament.

One time I ran across a Greek word *dokimadzo*. I looked it up in a lexicon and I found that it was a very significant word, and on further investigation I thought this word provided a clue to a practice in the early church, which has to a large extent been forgotten. *Dokimadzo* may be translated in various ways, sometimes "to discern" or "to prove," or sometimes it is translated "to test."

It reflects a practice in the early church according to which Christians would try to discern what the will of God was in relationship to the world in which they were. This was not just an individual or private practice when a person tried to know what was going on in the world, but it was something that was ordered into the very structure of the life and worship of the church.

Let me make reference to several passages where this appears. One of these is the very familiar passage in Romans 12:2, "Do not be conformed to this world, but be transformed by the renewal of your mind, that you may prove"—this could be translated "discern" or "test"—"what is the will of God, what is good and acceptable and perfect."

And when the apostle Paul wrote to the Philippian church he had a certain desire of them which was put into these words: "And it is my prayer that your love may abound more and more, with knowledge and all discernment, so that you may approve...." Then in 1 Thessalonians we hear this advice. "Do not quench the Spirit, do not despise prophesying, but test (or discern) everything: hold fast what is good."

WHAT IS GOD'S WILL?

Now all this says that it is necessary for the people of God to have some idea of what God's will is, and what is going on in the world. Now the N.T. people were Biblical Christians. They had, of course, only the O.T., and they used the O.T. as a clue to the meaning of history.

They were under the conviction, and rightly so, that the O.T. looked forward to the coming of Christ. This coming culminated in the resurrection and the ascension. But they were still in this world and they asked what the will of God was for them at that particular time.

For they were interested not only in the life of their own little fellowship but also in the course of history, and many references are made to their view of history in terms of principalities and powers.

Such terms are rather obscure to us in our day, but when we turn to Ephesians we read this: "for we are not contending against flesh and blood, but against the principalities and powers, against the world rulers of the present darkness, against the spiritual hosts of wickedness in the heavenly places."

This represents an outlook which most of us don't have. It was an outlook on the world, which included pantheons of angels and demons stretching from man up to God. It was a point of view shared by the pagan world.

Now the position that is taken in the Colossian letter is that Jesus has been victorious over all those principalities and powers. And yet at the same time, these principalities and powers are still alive as the power behind historical events. Even the decision of Pilate to crucify Jesus was a decision prompted by one of these principalities.

Now the approach of the early church to an understanding of history was one of trying to discern, under the influence of the Holy Spirit, what was going on in this world, what powers were behind the events, what was good and right, and what their place in the world was.

In other words, *discernment is the clue to N.T. ethics.* This means that they did not simply make logical deductions from certain good principles. They would look at an event in history and they would ask themselves as a community under the Holy Spirit, "What is the meaning of this? Is it good or bad? Is it for Christ or against Christ?" And that would be, to put it very simply, a criterion of right and wrong.

One of my pet questions when I go around to churches in New England is, "Well, what have you decided in the last year?" This question is most embarrassing. They decided to keep the minister for another year, to pay him a salary, and they made certain appointments of officers, and they are going to sustain the organization for one more year.

"But," I say, "what have you decided in terms of God's will, in terms of what this church should be doing in this world at this time, in terms of how to understand the course of history and how God may be related to it?" Now my feeling is that here we can learn much from the early church.

THE HOLY SPIRIT STILL INSPIRES

The people of the N.T. church accepted the responsibility of opening themselves to the inspiration of the Holy Spirit, and they opened their intelligence to the question of what was going on in the world at that time, and what their obligations to Christ and to the world were in the light of this.

Now, to put this more concretely, the time of the inspiration and the work of the Holy Spirit did not stop with the book of Revelation. The Bible is an authoritative and most useful avenue for the understanding of God's will, but it must be made contemporary only when we bring questions to it which come out of a contemporary situation.

There is nothing so deadly as just to study the Bible because it's the Bible. But if you bring real live questions to the Bible, then the Bible will in turn come alive, and it will speak and the Holy Spirit will guide in the understanding of the Bible.

The real problems, the important problems that confront society, must be discussed and studied by the church in the light of the Bible.

THE CONGREGATIONAL MEETING

How is it going to be done? I suggest the congregational meeting. Now that is a very simple idea and I get away with this idea in New England because there is an old tradition. The congregation meets at least once a month to discuss anything of importance.

This kind of meeting provides a natural time to come together as a congregation, and in all freedom and in openness to everyone present discuss what we think are the issues of the time, or what is now confronting a congregation.

This sounds simple, but there are many congregations in which problems have been brewing for 15 or 20 years. Through fear of trouble, they are never discussed, and are eventually settled by default.

They are forgotten but a lot of guilt and resentment remains. Now take for example, a civil rights problem in the South. One pastor was driven out of his church when he tried to get the church together to discuss the problem in their midst. It was talked about in the homes, in the restaurants, in the beer parlor, but it couldn't be talked about in the church.

Whenever a great social or theological problem cannot be talked about in the church, then I would say that the church has come under the power of one of those principalities. And the victory of Christ over that principality will come when Christ enables this community to have the freedom and openness to discuss this problem, looking hopefully to some sort of consensus.

We must provide the occasion when the issues can be brought out before the congregation for discussion. I should think that this might be done at congregational meetings.

I know of a church in New York City where they have a congregational meeting every month. The congregation stays after the eleven o'clock service on Sunday morning and into the afternoon for about two or three hours to discuss anything of importance. It dare not be trivial. They have a committee that decides whether a matter is important or trivial.

There is a sifting out of what are the great problems and then they concentrate on these. They are able to decide sometimes only about five or six things in a year, but they are basic.

I am contending that this is the work of the church. We sometimes think that the proper work of the church is what goes on Sunday mornings at eleven o'clock. That has become tradition. That's church, and anything else is sort of semi-church.

Without throwing out old patterns and practices it must be said that a congregation comes to order when it addresses itself under the inspiration of the Holy Spirit and with reference to the Bible to a great question. That is church in the very best sense of the word.

MUTUAL COUNSEL IN THE BODY OF CHRIST

There is something of this sort in the Anabaptist tradition. When I joined the church, I remember that the bishop asked me whether I would give counsel and receive counsel from others.

Well, I got a lot of counsel, but I never gave very much because I was never asked for very much. But there was a period in the church when this formula was taken very seriously. A person joining the church offered himself in terms of his counsel.

This means that one was open to God's direction so that one might be a contributing factor to the overall "discernment" of the congregation. And to give counsel meant that one must listen not merely out of democratic or personal respect for another person, but listen to that other person as one through whom God may speak.

This, of course, presupposes a dialogue and I am one who agrees with Franklin Littell, a friend of our tradition, in his claim that dialogue should have much more church and theological significance than it does.

We are inclined to think just like the Reformers that the way God speaks is through the preacher standing before an audience and preaching out of the Bible. Now, I can agree with that, but that is not the only way God may speak. He may speak through the dialectic as you might say of the "yes" and "no."

On almost any important question a congregation will be divided to start with, and we may deplore this. Frankly, it is nothing to deplore at all. That is just recognition of the fact that we are historical beings. We all look at things from a point of view. We are all prejudiced and especially those who claim they are not prejudiced.

None of us are objective, but I have been in enough of these sessions to realize that often a discussion, which begins with two or three points of view, can be far more colorful and productive than if all agree to start with.

And I wonder whether there might not be a stage in this discussion when God is pleased with contradictory answers if the group is committed to the truth that lies beyond any one person, and if it is ready to speak tentatively, looking for a solution down the line.

I think it is not only a matter of etiquette or group dynamics to suggest that when a problem is raised, it might be good for a person to say with a certain tentativeness, "Well, this is the way it seems to me," rather than say, "This is the way it is," and then dig in.

LOVING, OPEN ATMOSPHERES ESSENTIAL

We need an atmosphere in which we can say, "This is what I believe," as well as back off without losing face, without losing one's ego. In the best Quaker tradition people listened to God through the other person and realized that the truth is more likely to come out in consensus at the end rather than in the individual statements, which have been made.

If we could only create in our churches an atmosphere of freedom, an openness, so that even the young people get up and say something, so that a person can be found to be wrong and still be in good standing in every respect—if we could only create that kind of atmosphere, then we would be in a position to move.

There is real theological value in consensus. I am not ready to say that every congregational consensus must *ipso facto* be the will of God. That is just a little too easy. But I would say our congregations ought to move forward, hope for, and pray for consensus on all-important issues involving the congregation as a whole. And when they come to a consensus, they have something to rejoice about. Now, of course, one matter for wisdom is to decide what calls for consensus and what does not.

A CHURCH MAY CHANGE ITS MIND

Of course, someone may say, "Well, what if you can't get consensus?"

Well, then, you can't get consensus. But at least the congregation knows that it doesn't agree, which is a very good thing. In this case the congregation must make a place for loyal dissent.

After all, it is conceivable that the minority dissenters may be right. This will allow for a certain openness toward the day when the congregation may have to change its mind.

And what I would like to find on the face of the earth is a religious body that can change its mind, and change it honestly and openly with a kind of sense of humor about itself.

For it is a fact that history moves and the church moves, and the church has to make up its mind. In the Catholic Church, even popes have had to change their minds. That's an embarrassment to the Catholic Church. But Catholics have no monopoly on this.

Historically, church bodies have had a hard time changing their minds, and I think it is partly because we tend to ascribe a false deity to ourselves. We hesitate to confess that we may have been wrong at one time for fear someone would raise some question about the nature of the church.

Actually I think we will stand much better if we can admit that the church has an element of humanity in it, and that therefore the church can make mistakes and may need to change its mind. There is no need to apologize for this; the necessity is to make changes that are called for graciously.

DISCERNMENT AND UNITY

The discerning community is that community which raises fundamental questions and has a method within itself whereby it can come to conclusions and then act upon them.

Unfortunately we often deal with problems which are not our own. We employ our denominational people to think up problems for us and to write materials about them, and then we try to take over problem and material. But actually both are second-hand.

The way to be real is to have problems emerge right out of our midst, and any church that is in mission is going to have these kinds of problems. But some may say, "Aren't you inviting disunity into the church if you bring things out into the open like this? Can you really have peace in the church?"

My answer is that we must redefine our concept of peace. Peace within the brotherhood is not an absence of differences, not even the absence of tensions. Peace is the condition, is the dynamic or resolving tensions, a reconciliation of people who are involved in these tensions. And a church, which has no tensions, no problems, and no possibilities of division, is a dead church. It just means that it is not really facing its problems.

Controversial questions are often the important questions, and controversial questions should be brought before the church. And if the church can't handle controversial questions, then it is under the domination of principalities and powers.

It is astounding that it is possible to talk about important national/political issues on radio, television, or the Internet; and possible *everywhere* but in church. It is a bad thing when such vital issues can't be talked about. That means that the church is paralyzed by this demon, this principality that we call "politics."

And the victory of Christ is that freedom which enables us to look out on this world and be in a position under the Holy Spirit to pass judgment on anything or anybody. That is the kind of freedom the church must enjoy. Instead of that, we are afraid of being divided and therefore we won't look at controversial questions. The fact is, controversy, if it is loving controversy, can be very enlightening and can help us.

This article originally appeared in *Searching Together,* 16:1, Spring, 1987.

"When I ask myself the main reason for so many people having left the church during the past decades in France, Germany, Holland, and also in Canada and America, the word "power" easily comes to mind. One of the greatest ironies of the history of Christianity is that its leaders constantly gave in to the temptation of power—political power, military power, economic power, or moral and spiritual power—even though they continued to speak in the name of Jesus, who did not cling to his divine power but emptied himself and became as we are."

—**Henri Nouwen**, *In the Name of Jesus*, p. 75

CHAPTER 16

I HAVE LEFT YOU AN EXAMPLE: AUTHORITY IN SERVANTHOOD

Jon Zens

"Authority" is one of the most controversial issues in the church today. It is a very practical matter for many have been severely wounded and disillusioned by the misuse of authority, and properly defining and submitting to Christ's authority is of the utmost concern to the Christian conscience.

When I compare the traditional view of authority in the church[1] with what is revealed in the New Testament, I see little resemblance between the two. A fresh examination of what the N.T. teaches on authority is certainly called for in light of the assumption that traditional views of authority are correct.[2]

Such an examination is also warranted because of the perverted notions of authority being practiced that are foreign to the N.T. Church leaders take it upon themselves to tell the flock what to eat, when to shower, when to fast, where to move, etc. A pastor tells the flock Sunday night that beards, mustaches and hair over the ears are suspect, and by Wednesday's prayer meeting all the men appear with army haircuts and no facial hair. A "Bible-believing" group in New England justifies child beatings on the authority of Proverbs 13:24. In one church, the members must notify the elders beforehand if they are going to miss the Sunday meetings. Failure to do this opens the door to church discipline. A pastor's wife informs the church that God has revealed to her that all birth control is evil, and within a month most of the church's women are pregnant. One church makes *not* having a T.V. a condition of membership.

What does the N.T. teach? The study of a Biblical word usually reveals that you cannot put it in a box. But one thing is for sure: *the traditional ideas about "authority" in the church are generally detached from the N.T.'s presentation.* Certain N.T. patterns are obvious and must shape our view of authority.

A BASIC DEFINITION OF AUTHORITY

The Greek word for "authority" is *exousia*. It comes from the verb *exestin*, which means:

1. "that an action is possible in the sense that there are no hindrances... 'to be able'"

2. "that an action is not prevented by a higher norm"[3]

Exousia, then, means the right to do something or the right over something.[4] With reference to God, authority is absolute and unchallengeable (Luke 12:5; Rom. 9:21). God can grant or delegate authority in various ways (Rev. 6:8; 14:18). The *exousia* of Satan falls into this category (Job 1:12; 2:5-6).

The church has "authority," but it is *derived* from Christ's action on her behalf. Christ "gives" the keys of the kingdom to the church. In Christ the church has *exousia*, or "freedom", (1 Cor. 8:9). But this freedom is to be used for the welfare of others, and not for self-gratification. Christ possesses all authority, and this has significant implications for the expression of "authority" among Christ's people: authority is manifested through the sacrificial giving of one's life for others, and by admonishing one another with God's Word. When authority is said to reside in persons because of their "position," the way is clear for self-exaltation and the teaching of human rules.

NEW TESTAMENT PATTERNS OF AUTHORITY

1. *Actual (intrinsic) authority rests in the person of Christ.* All *exousia* has been given to the Son by the Father (Matt. 28:18). Christ's earthly ministry can generally be subsumed under three headings:

   A. a purposeful gathering ministry

   B. a powerful sign ministry

   C. a positive teaching ministry

   In each of these His authority is prominent. In *gathering people,* He has the authority to call them, save them, forgive them, and gift/grace them for service (John 17:2; Matt. 9:6,8; Eph. 4:7,11,16). In *miracles,* His authority over the devil, the natural elements, diseases, etc., is manifest (Matt. 10:1; 8:27; Mark 1:27; 4:41). In *teaching,* His words carry authority (Matt. 7:29; 18:20).

2. *Christ delegates authority to His servants,* (Matt. 10:1; Mark 13:34; Luke 19:17). In light of Christ's absolute authority, it becomes apparent that any "authority" expressed among His people *cannot* reside in a person or persons *inherently* (or intrinsically). It can only be a *derivative* authority. Since the One with all authority (John 13:3) clearly gave the directive for how "greatness" in the kingdom would be attained (Matt. 20:26-27), authority in the church must be in line with Christ's example.

   Most probably think of authority as attached to being in an "office." But where does the N.T. teach this? Authority in the church—the ability to do something—comes as the body *recognizes how a person has been functioning.*

There is certainly no evidence that the kind of authority described in Matt. 8:9—"I say to one, 'Go,' and he goes; and to another 'Come, and he comes"—is ever applied to leadership in the church. In fact, Christ's reference to the way unbelieving rulers exercise authority over others is excluded as a model in His kingdom: "not so among you" (Matt. 20:26).

3. *Christ's model for authority in the church is opposite to the way unbelieving societies function.* (Matt. 20:25-35; Mark 9:33-35; 10:37-45; Luke 9:48; 22:25; John 13:14-15; 18:36; 19:10-11). Authority is exercised in Christ's domain by being the slave of others, not by being the master over others. Even though Christ forbids the church to copy the world in this regard, the visible church has more often than not modeled herself after the power structures of worldly governments and corporations.

   Paul in his service for Christ was very concerned to *never* "lord it over" the faith of others (2 Cor. 1:24; 1 Cor. 2:1-5). Peter exhorts the elders not to "lord it over God's flock" (who are the *kleron*, or "clergy"; 1 Pet. 5:3). The *power* associated with traditional "offices" has not fostered obedience to this apostolic mandate.

4. *Authority among Christ's people is expressed in servanthood, with a view toward the welfare and edification of others,* (Matt. 10:8; 1 Cor. 8:9; 2 Cor. 10:8; 13:10). We tend to think of authority in terms of "the guy on the top" or "the one who has the final word" (like the world does). But in Christ's domain, authority comes by being at the feet of others (Mark 9:33-35; 2 Cor. 11:23-33). Indeed, Jesus rules in an "upside-down kingdom"![5]

5. *Influence among Christ's people cannot be authoritarian (intrinsic); it must be authoritative (extrinsic).* Christ as the final voice in the church, rules it through His Word. Thus all in the church—including leaders—are subject to the same Head. The authority in the church, therefore, is *extrinsic,* that is, the authority is *outside* of the members, and does not reside inherently (or because of "office") in any one or more of the members. This alone restrains authoritarianism, for in such relationships people usurp Christ's Headship and act as though authority rests in them.

   Submission to others (wives to husbands, children to parents, flock to overseers) is always *with respect to Christ, not in the place of Christ.* The importance of this can be seen in the marriage relationship. Wives are commanded to submit to their husbands, but this in no way implies that there is not a mutual dimension to marriage. Paul says in 1 Corinthians 7:4 that neither husband nor wife has "authority" over their bodies; rather, the bodies of each belong to the other. Hence they are not to withdraw sexually from one another unless it is done—not by a unilateral decree by the husband—but by mutual "agreement" (Greek, *Sumphonou;* "symphony").

6. *There are "authorities" (exousiai; which we call governments or earthly powers) to which Christians submit themselves.* But they too are under Christ's Lordship and cannot be obeyed when they command what Christ forbids, or forbid what Christ commands (Acts 5: 29; Rom. 13:1-3; Eph. 1:21; 2:2; 3:10; 6:12; (Col. 2:10,15; Titus 3:1).

State "power" is not absolute. For various reasons the *exousia* in Roman 13:1ff has been virtually equated with *God's* authority, as if most state actions have His approval or sanction. But we must remember that Satan has a derived *exousia*, which obviously is not under God's blessing—although He does *permit* it, (Luke 4:6; Acts 26:18; Job 1:12; 2:6).

God does not hallow and consecrate the civil authority; such hallowing is reserved for the Messianic community. But he does allot to the civil authorities a place, a role; they too, even in their covert violence or their raging, are not outside of His ordering of all things in this fallen world.

Relevant also is the fact that Nero was Emperor when (Rom.13) was written. It is not said that God bestows on the *exousia* a divine consecration, but rather that He assigns it a place, a role.[6]

In light of the N.T. patterns, our definition and conception of "authority" in the church need to be re-evaluated. The traditional concept of "authority" emphasizes the "over others" aspect, which characterizes the worldly outlook, and has the practical effect of "limiting" others. Exousia in Christ's church is not reached by being personally "over" others, but by being at the disposal of others to meet their needs.

Notes for "Example"

1   *Cf.* James L Ainslie, "The Powers of the Reformed Ministerial Order," The Doctrines of the Ministerial Order in the Reformed churches of the 16th and 17th Centuries (T & T Clark, 1940), 62-90; Marjorie Warkentin, "Authority & Ordination," *Ordination: A Biblical-Historical View* (Eerdmans, 1982), 173-183: James Bannerman. "The Ministry A Divine & Standing Ordinance in the Church," The Church of Christ, Vol.1, 421-435

2. This fact is highlighted, for example, in an interview with four "clergymen" about "authority and power" in the church. They assume that the status quo notions about authority are a given, and are seemingly oblivious to what the N.T. says about authority. ("Power, Preaching & Priorities," Leadership: Power & Authority, 1:1, Winter 1980, 11-28)

3. W. Foerester, "Exestin, Exousia, etc.," Theological Dictionary of the New Testament, ed. G Kittel, Vol.2, p. 560

4. Ibid., p. 562

5   *Cf.* Donald Kraybill, The Upside-Down Kingdom (Herald, 1978).

6. Dale Aukerman, Darkening Valley: A Biblical Perspective on Nuclear War (Seabury, 1981), 95,97.

This article originally appeared in *Searching Together,* 13:1, Spring, 1984.

"So that you obey the bishop and the presbytery with an undivided mind . . ."

—**Ignatius**, *To the Ephesians*, Chapter 20

"Apart from the bishop no one is to do anything pertaining to the church."

—**Ignatius**

CHAPTER 17
CAN 'LAYMEN' QUESTION?

R.L. Wysong

*(**Editor's Note** – Although the author in this book is dealing with the creation/evolution debate, the observations he makes in this chapter apply to the intimidation created and sustained by the "clergy/laity" distinction. The N.T. teaches that all of God's children are laity ("people") and clergy ("inheritance"). But the deep-rooted tradition views the "layman" as (basically) ignorant, and hence the need for a "learned" clergy. Jesus taught that wisdom comes from babes, not from the "Dr.'s" of this age (cf. 1 Cor. 1:26-27). Humble "laymen" often have more insight than hardened "clergy.")*

Dogmatic and authoritative pronouncements fulminate from both religious and evolutionary camps. The layman is intimidated. He asks, *"Who am I to question recognized authority?"* The man on the street, fearing some sort of ostracism or humiliation if he dare raise his voice as a skeptic, simply allows himself to be swept along by the edicts—the course of least resistance.

In this chapter we will consider the propriety of laymen entering the controversy and deciding for themselves in a reasonable way the truth on origins. This will require sifting through some of the more popular argumentation foisted on the public and encouraging individuals to dissect and openly challenge dogma.... We will necessarily generalize and speak of two categories, religion and evolution, but not all that we say will apply to all evolutionists or all religionists. And, since there are many in religion that accept evolution and many evolutionists who accept religion, this categorization is artificial and is not meant to set up a rigid dichotomy. The intent of this expose is simply to reveal attitudes we must watch out for in our pursuit of truth on origins.

ARE CREDENTIALS NECESSARY?
Are we audacious in feeling that we, as "laymen," can resolve the controversy? There are those who would say so. Some feel this controversy is open game only

for theologians with "proper" credentials. We simply don't have the proper schooling, they may say. So the argument is that the laity must have tacit faith and trust the pronouncements of those religiously qualified. But why so? The original "theologians" were lay people. If they could formulate creationistic concepts, we need no special credentials to challenge or validate them. Issues that affect us personally should be resolved personally...

Further justification for the jury members in the court of origins being laymen lies with the realization...that origins have far reaching impact upon human activity. Origins are not merely an academic matter; they are not an esoteric abstruse philosophical problem fit only to be ricocheted back and forth between the minds of mental giants in university or theological conclaves. Origins affect you and me through their effect upon education, politics, sociology, psychology, and individual, man-on-the-street philosophy and ethics. This makes the subject of origins open game for Joe Public.

In this regard, Marshall and Sandra Hall wrote:

> Who is to say, after all, that ordinary citizens don't have the right to question any group of experts if that group's actions affect the entire spectrum of everybody's life, young, old, working or at leisure?.... If atomic scientists make some little slip and wipe out Oregon, are citizens from neighboring states to allow new atomic sites to be built near them because they feel unqualified as non-scientists in making such a decision, (*The Truth: God or Evolution* (Craig, 1974), p. 99.

ARGUMENT FROM "EXPERT" TESTIMONY

Expert testimonials are a common crutch for the limp in one's ability to muster a rational argument. Creationists often cite theologians or scientists as experts "proving" their position....

Evolutionists agree to the historicity, actuality, reality and fact of evolution. There is, however, no consensus on the exact mechanism by which the process took place. Thus we will find evolutionary expert vying with evolutionary expert on all facets of the proposed evolutionary scheme. Apropos are the words of Hilaire Belloc:

> But scientists who ought to know.
>
> Assure us that it must be so...
>
> Oh! Let us never, never doubt
>
> What nobody is sure about.

If a layman were to choose to disagree with both sides of a given point, would he then be a naïve, credulous, moronic, uninformed imbecile? Certainly not, for he could cite "experts" that reject either side; thus, the layman would have expert backing....

1. If expert A disagrees with expert B on a given point

2. And expert B disagrees with expert A on the same point

3. Then laymen can disagree with A and have the backing of B, and also disagree with B and have the backing of A

4. Thus laymen can disagree with both of the experts on the same point in question and have expert backing in so doing

Does this discussion mean we cannot use any testimonials from experts? No. We simply mean that an expert's interpretation of the facts, his conclusions, taken alone and detached from reason, should not be sufficiently convincing. It is, of course, proper to cite experts to establish facts and acquaint us with evidence and, if necessary, counter an opposing expert testimony.

ARGUMENT FROM POPULARITY

Truth is never determined on the basis of a popularity poll. Citing this scholar or that one as holding beliefs similar to ours is tenuous support. The argument from popularity *(argumentum ad populum)* is logically invalid.

We often hear statements to the effect that the entire scientific community believes in the fact of evolution. Or, in the past era, theologians could argue the same about creationism. Pronouncements from popularity convey impact on the layman and have the effect of deadening inquiry. Few wish to be unique, odd, renegades or intellectual dropouts. So, in self-defense, laymen side with whatever is vogue.

Tactics based upon group pressure—popularity—are also the basis for many of the commercials we encounter daily: since everyone is doing it, eating it, using it, buying it and believing it, shouldn't you? Children especially feel the pressure from the slogan, "everybody's doing it," as evidenced by the fads in dress, drugs, language and morals.

Surely the gimmickry in advertising is obvious, and the naïve need for acceptance by the crowd is expected of children; but should mature thinkers succumb? Certainly not, for under the guise of popularity and authoritarian pressure is cheap advertising and tactics fit only to convince impressionable youth.

POPULARITY IN REVERSE

Up until the present century, creationism held the upper hand in terms of popularity. But now evolution is secured by the vote of the masses—at least the educated masses. So the argument that the entire scientific community believes it is now commonly heard. But this is not true, and even if it were, of what value is the argument?

Although it is true that most in academia believe evolution, there are not an insignificant number who hold the opposite position, or at least have rejected evolution.... So we could say that there is definitely a growing popularity in reverse. But we could also say, "so what!" Exactly—popularity means nothing regardless of what side it is on.

PROPAGANDA

Religionists have been noted for their submission to propaganda and blind faith. Dogmatic statements of doctrine are thundered from the pulpits and the laity is to acquiesce. The faithful are even asked not to entertain contrary views in literature or discussion. If one questions accepted doctrine, if he finds it weak under close scrutiny, he throws his "spirituality" and "faith" into question. Answers like "have faith my son" or "it is a divine mystery" are foisted as adequate rebuttal to any challenge. Thus reason and the rational approach are abandoned. Propaganda is substituted.

It is interesting how religionists will argue against the use of reason through the use of reason. This is like arguing that shovels are a contemptible tool, condemning them by putting all the world's shovels in a large hole and covering them over with dirt shoveled in by a shovel!

Everyone will press reason into service when, by so doing, they can bolster their own cherished beliefs. But when reason contradicts preconceived ideas, reason is forsaken and even turned upon. If reason is of no value, or only limited worth, then all men would be led to universal skepticism. No system of thought, religious or secular, could stand....

If one dares to challenge traditional teachings, counter arguments and castigations will often follow this general line:

1. One must assume the doctrine as true before examining the facts

2. Contrary facts are deemed not properly understood, shelved as mysteries and thought of as tests of faith

3. That which is popular must be true

4. Appropriate credentials (obtained by being selectively trained—propagandized—in a sanctioned religious school) are prerequisites to discussion, criticism, or free thought on religious matters

5. The search for supporting evidences must be made by neglecting the material, which might crimp the proof

To be sure, in the minds of many, those who consider the creation alternative are a reproachful lot. In the minds of others, those who consider evolution are likewise reproachful. But an intolerant attitude is merely a symptom of the age-old "follow the crowd" syndrome. To many, nonconformity in itself is sufficient reason to heap reproach on another.

Rickover wrote of those who dare to go against the stream:

The 'controversial' tag makes him a 'flawed' personality, not group-adjusted, one-sided, ill informed, frustrated and motivated by ill will. Epithets may therefore be thrown at him with impunity; he may be misquoted and misrepresented, and what he says may be contemptuously dismissed as requiring no refutation whatever, (H.G. Rickover, "Decline of the Individual," *Saturday Evening Post*, #236, March 30, 1963, p. 11).

NECESSITY OF CRITICISM

Both creationists and evolutionists believe they have the truth. A quality of truth is its ability to hold up under criticism. But some in religion feel it improper to even raise questions, much less criticize, what is traditional. Some evolutionists also insulate their views from critical probings.

To win men to the truth, their minds must be won. Minds are not won by dogmatism. Dogmatism produces, at best, menial robots. Minds are won by openness.

When the scientific community originally accepted Darwin's ideas, they did so to be emancipated from religion's intellectually stifling effects.... The authors, Marshall and Sandra Hall, wrote:

> Organized religion's record of intolerance and superstition drives many people to accept evolutionary answers.... Up to then, those who had turned away from organized religion had done so primarily as a reaction against the corruption, intolerance, and often cruelty of the Roman Catholic Church; defects often equaled in the 16th through 19th Centuries by the Protestants. Thus out of reaction against the rigidity of the Church, and fortified by science in their doubts relating to church dogma, many were ripe indeed for the 'book that shook the world,' [*Origin of Species: God or Evolution*, pp. 5, 98, 122].

On the other hand, many evolutionists are now simply repeating the mentality of religions that originally drove them to their position....

Without investigation and criticism discovery stops. If evolutionism suppresses its critics, then its status as a science is questionable. On the other hand, if religion suppresses critics, then it cannot be the vicar of truth it claims to be.

Truth welcomes deliberate criticism, perusal, inspection, scrutiny and review. If evolution is true, or creation is true, they should bare themselves to this action....

A faith built upon a solid rational foundation invites criticism and refinement; faith built upon a bubble jealously protects itself from the ravages of attack for fear it may burst.

If truth is our goal, why not open our views to close scrutiny? If we have the truth, our views will stand; if we don't, let them fall.

SUPPRESSION OF HERETICS

Unfortunately the intimidation of the layman has often been extended beyond propagandizing and gentle authoritarian nudges. In some cases it has become outright persecution and suppression.

In the past, especially, religions viciously and mercilessly attacked dissenting individuals. A noteworthy example is the Inquisition. Cruelty, torture, sadism and ostracism have all been done in the spirit of "truth preservation."

Religion has lost much of her power. Today evolutionists have it. And surprisingly they are known to use the same inquisitorial tactics against heretics. It is deemed apostate by some evolutionary minds to even mention creationism as a possible alternative. If creation is considered one might suspect his ability to walk and chew bubble gum at the same time.

Abundant are the sad stories of students who have pursued advanced degrees, only to be denied them because they rejected evolutionism... Has freedom of the press become the freedom to be sure that all of the propaganda is on one side, and a free land a place where you can say what you think if the majority thinks the same thing?

Society today is very concerned about human rights and equality. There is the black movement, the Chicano movement, gay liberation, women's liberation, student liberation, and child liberation. The need for freedom to express individuality seems to be keenly before the public. Why cannot such freedoms be extended to laymen who wish to rationally consider the topic of origins? Does the fact that a religious world once suppressed freedom of thought and scientific inquiry justify the scientific community's like action today?

Those who cling to their doctrines in a cynical way have no true foundation for what they believe, and avoid discussion, criticism, or thought on the matter. Both the religionist and evolutionist, who display these attitudes, are in dangerous positions. For without inquiry, criticism and thought, one has no real assurance that his convictions are valid. Our lives could be revolving around a philosophical lie. Truth is our goal. We have only to gain from searching it out and reconciling ourselves to it.

So, *can laymen question?* Yes! They have every right. The layman should be able to see that the expert testimonials, *argumentum ad populum,* propaganda, and suppression are flimsy, specious substitutes for rational arguments.... If we are to be intimidated, let's let the evidence do it.

This article originally appeared in *Searching Together,* 13:1, Spring, 1984.

CHAPTER 18
PRIESTHOOD, EUCHARIST & ORDINATION

A Review Article by Jon Zens

Is there a clear N.T. pattern and authority for perpetuating these [traditional] structures, or do they actually stifle the intended function and ministry of the church?

—James D.G. Dunn

The Summer 1981 Baptist Reformation Review (now *Searching Together*) *(S.T.)* contained selected comments of William Barclay on 1 Corinthians 14. Barclay was a N.T. scholar of wide repute (although the evangelical community would find his views on some items, e.g. miracles, repugnant). Though Barclay himself was a member of the very formal and liturgical Church of Scotland, when he faced Paul's remarks in 1 Corinthians 14 he found a very different practice of "church":

> 1 Corinthians 14 sheds a flood of light on what a church service was like in the early Church. There was obviously a freedom and informality about it, which is completely strange to our ideas.... Clearly the early Church had no professional ministry.... There was obviously a flexibility about the order of service, which is now totally lacking.... The really notable thing about an early Church service must have been that almost everyone came feeling that he had both the privilege and the obligation of contributing something to it.... The Church must have been in those days much more the real possession of the ordinary Christian.[1]

In *New Testament Theology in Dialogue*[2] Catholic John Mackey and Protestant James D.G. Dunn discuss important issues related to Christology and Ministry. Dunn is regarded as one of the foremost contemporary N.T. scholars.[3] His books, *Baptism In the Holy Spirit, Jesus and the Spirit, Unity and Diversity in the N.T., An Inquiry into the Characteristics of the Earliest Christianity, Jesus, Paul and the Law,* and his two volume commentary on Romans are each monumental and significant studies.

Given the scholarly acumen of Dunn, it fascinates me to see what he considers the N.T. evidence regarding "Priesthood," "Eucharist" (Lord's Supper), and "Ordination." In *New Testament Theology in Dialogue* (pp. 121-140), he arrives at the same basic conclusions we have suggested in *ST* over the years. I would like to review Dunn's assessment of the N.T. data in these three areas, and suggest certain implications for those of us in the body of Christ today.

PRIESTHOOD

Dunn freely acknowledges that post-apostolic Christian history has centered on the functions of the "clergy" and admits that "no one really knows yet what 'the ministry of the whole people of God' amounts to" (p. 121). At a minimum, this highlights the fact that traditional treatments on church practice are lopsided. The "priesthood of all believers" is a field ripe for further investigation in the light of N.T. information.

A distinctive of the N.T., asserts Dunn, "is the complete absence from its pages of a distinction between 'priest' and 'laity,' of the thought that some Christians may or must needs exercise a priesthood which is not the prerogative of others" (p. 122). This N.T. viewpoint, he notes, "marks it off both from the O.T. and from what was subsequently to become the pattern of Catholic Christianity (p.122). Compared to the Jewish and Greco-Roman religions surrounding them, "the first Christian congregations were an oddity indeed—religious groups without priest or sacrifice" (p. 123).

In the Third and Fourth centuries a separate class of "clergy" was viewed as indispensable, but it "never occurred to the first Christian churches and writers that a priest was necessary for the functioning of the church as a church or desirable for its well-being" (p. 124).

The fact that so much emphasis came to rest on the "clergy"—a separate order within the ranks of believers—probably accounts in large part for why direct relationship with Christ seemed so distant and clouded to the people in the pew. "Those who yearn for a priesthood of the old kind, like the order of Aaron," Dunn suggests, "are in danger of falling back into the era of shadows and imperfection, and of losing the immediacy of that communion with God which it was Christ's whole purpose to bring about" (p. 125).

The emergence of a clergy-class also contributed to the mistaken notion that the Christian life was divided into two parts—the "sacred" and the "profane."

The N.T. concept of priesthood sees all Christians as offering "their lives in the ordinary physical involvement of everyday commerce and intercourse. The cult has been desacralized. Or, better, everyday life has been sanctified" (p. 127). The priestly function of all "was retained precisely by breaking down the barrier between cult and everyday life, between priest and laity" (p. 128).

But because of the traditional ideas connected to clergy functions, the mind-set persists that there are "holy" (sacred) and "ordinary" (profane) professions. For this reason, Dunn points out, "some of the early statements regarding industrial chaplaincies...seemed to imply that the Church was not present in industry unless and until an ordained clergyman became involved on the factory floor" (p. 127). Dunn knows that there is virtually no correlation in practice between the priesthood of all believers articulated in the N.T. and the post-Constantinian church. He sees the implications of this as a matter of grave concern.

> When Clement resorted once again to the distinction between 'priest' and 'laity' (1 Clem. 40:5), he was pointing down a road, which would fundamentally compromise, if not make a mere cipher of, a very basic element in earliest Christianity's self-understanding.... It is the apparent disregard for something quite so fundamental by subsequent Christian history that does more to undermine the canonical authority of the N.T. than most heresies.... The major authority acknowledged by all Christians (the N.T.) has been effectively discounted and ignored. (pp. 126, 128-129).

THE LORD'S SUPPER

As clergy came increasingly into the spotlight, it is easy to see how the administration of baptism and the Eucharist became their special assignment. In this regard, the 'priest' in Roman Catholicism differed little in essence from the 'minister' in Protestantism.

> 'New Presbyter is but old priest writ large' (Milton). The crucial factor being, once again, the fact that only ordained clergy may preside at the Eucharist... The fact that only the ordained minister can preside at Holy Communion meant that it all comes to the same thing, the ordained clergyman (or clergyperson) is exercising a priesthood distinct in essence from the priesthood of all (p.129)

Clearly, "the breaking of bread and drinking of wine in remembrance of Christ was an established feature of the Christian churches from the start" (p.130). However, in the N.T. there is no thought of a "ministerial priesthood to validate participation of the Supper" (p.131).

One simple reason why there was no thought given in the N.T. to the need of a clergy-person to preside was the fact that the Supper was a shared meal, not a "sacrament" (p.131). Dunn notes that the "fellowship reality of the new covenant was to be expressed in a common meal whose significance came to focus in the words spoken by Jesus over the bread and one of the cups" (p.131).

Dunn suggests that, "given...the common meal as the context of the Lord's Supper within the N.T., it needs to be considered whether the separation of the Eucharist into a ritual act on its own has lost something of major importance in the existence and practice of Christian community " (p.133).

Also, it is interesting to note that this separation combined with the "reemergence of an order of priesthood...mark the loss of a dimension of fellowship, common participation which was a central feature of Christian beginnings" (p.133).

One radical aspect of the new covenant was the setting aside of "holy places" (John 4:20-24). "There was no such thing as a 'sacred space' for these first Christians" (p.134). Thus, a distinguishing mark of the early church was that they had no religious buildings for their meetings. They met in a setting where meals were natural.

> What this meant in practice is that the first Christian congregations met in homes—home churches. In these circumstances the context of the Eucharist was likely to be the meal table in the home.... When the Lord's Supper was celebrated, it would have been the host(ess) who in the course of the common meal reminded his or her guests of the words first said by Jesus on the night on which he was betrayed (pp. 134, 135).

ORDINATION

In traditional views of the church, it is ordination, which constitutes the essential difference between clergy and laity (p. 136). It is the official recognition ordination gives that empowers the clergy to "administer the sacraments." Dunn readily admits that there is a concept of ordination in the N.T. (pp. 136-137). The N.T. has no problem with the idea of recognizing and "setting apart" various ministries by the laying of hands. But he quickly adds:

> However, this conclusion must be integrated into our earlier findings.... What is in mind in such N.T. passages cannot be the same understanding of ordination as that which constitutes a priest and marks off one form of ministry as "essentially different" from all other ministry.... It may be legitimately asked from the N.T. side of the dialogue whether any concept of ordination, which divides Christian ministry into two kinds, can be justified (p.137).

He also observes that passages speaking of ordination refer to short-term ministries on a number of occasions (p. 139). Dunn concludes by making these pointed observations about N.T. ordination:

> The fundamental ordination is the gift of the Spirit to all who believe; and the diversities of ministry, which ensue, are no different in kind from one another.... There is much to be said (in the N.T.) for a broader concept of ordination and for different kinds of ordination, and much against the traditional concepts of ministry and ordination.... To begin to categorize grace into different classes, qualitatively different in character and effectiveness, is a fearful step for a follower of Jesus to take. And to narrow the channels of grace in the way the classical theory of ordination does, seems to be an attempt to recreate the very form of religion which Jesus and the N.T. writers seem to have been reacting against, and to have rejoiced at leaving behind in their sense of eschatological fulfillment, (pp. 138, 139).

Dunn's survey of the N.T. data in the three areas under consideration leaves us with the following major points:

1. The clergy/laity distinction, which developed in the post-apostolic tradition is unknown in the N.T.

2. In the N.T. ministry and grace belong to the whole people of God, with great diversity among the parts for the common good of all.

3. There is no overriding focus in the N.T. on a special class of ministry granted only to the "ordained".

4. The whole life of every believer is a "liturgy" offered in response to God's redemptive work in Christ, (Rom.12:1-2). Worship is all of life for both the elder in the assembly and the carpenter in the shop.

5. The clergy-tradition, along with the attendant host of practices built upon it, has probably done more to undermine N.T. authority in the church than most heresies.

6. The various ministries intended for all believers have been stifled by the creation of, and almost exclusive focus on, the special caste of the "ordained." Whether "priest" in Catholicism or "pastor" in Protestantism the result is the same: significant and necessary ministry is perceived as limited to those who fill the historically defined role expectations of "the minister."

7. The New Testament nowhere limits the baptizing of believers to the "ordained."

8. In the early church the Lord's Supper was in the context of a shared meal. Thus, the idea of needing an "official" person to preside over an alleged "sacrament" was unnecessary and totally foreign to the ethos of the N.T.

9. The early assemblies that appeared in connection with gospel preaching were very unusual compared to all the religions that surrounded them. They had no assigned places, no "sacred" buildings outside of their homes designated as "holy places." Also, they did not have a class of religious experts, a separate "priesthood" to officiate.

10. By reverting to the Old Testament concept of the exclusive priesthood of a few, the church has unwittingly (sometimes knowingly) capitulated to religious patterns alien to the new covenant, and as a result lost "a dimension of fellowship (and) common participation which was a central feature of Christian beginnings," (p.133).

LINGERING THOUGHTS & QUESTIONS

Are we willing to evaluate our practices in light of the simplicity concerning what "church" really is as described in the N.T.?

What does it mean to listen to the N.T concerning what "church is about? In light of the N.T. data regarding the "church," how do we prove that we are doers and not hearers only?

How can we claim to take the N.T. seriously as our "rule of faith and practice," and yet turn a deaf ear to clear, undeniable patterns of body life unfolded therein?

If our practice contradicts the N.T., why do we keep affirming that the N.T. is our infallible guide? Why don't we just admit that we really do not care what the N.T. says, and we prefer our inherited way of doing things?

What would happen in most existing churches if the N.T "texts could be allowed to speak in their own terms without the filter of denominational tradition and centuries-old vested interest." (p. 140)

Is it not easy to reach the conclusion that most church structures do not cultivate or enhance N.T. concerns and goals for Christ's people?

Dunn marks the undeniable shift that took place in post-apostolic history:

Increasing institutionalism is the clearest mark of early Catholicism—when church becomes increasingly identified with institution, when authority becomes increasingly coterminous with office, when a basic distinction between clergy and laity becomes increasingly self-evident, when grace becomes increasingly narrowed to well defined ritual acts. We saw above that such features were absent from first generation Christianity; though in the second generation the picture was beginning to change.[5]

I have never seen a N.T. scholar from any theological tradition deny this shift from early simplicity and polyform ministry to institutionalism and uniform ministry. If this shift brought inestimable harm to gospel unity and mutual care in the body, is it not incumbent for each of us to seriously examine ourselves and ask: "In my practice of 'church' am I contributing to the perpetuation of unedifying traditions, or am I giving myself to edifying N.T. principles which will serve as caring models for future generations?" To the degree that we allow the status quo to go on unchallenged and unquestioned, we stand intensely accountable to our Lord Jesus Christ. The ecclesiastical systems in place for hundreds of years have multiplied church splits, and crushed, wounded, trampled upon, stifled and even killed the dearest people. Does such unparalleled harm not grieve your heart and serve as a call to action out of love to Christ and His people?

The Christian institutions of our day have a way of intimidating people. The organized churches of our day are often large, tenured, and based on the same kind of power structures that characterize secular organizations. As a result, it is not easy to implement changes, or to seek to do things in ways that are more in line with the simplicity of the N.T. pattern. Those who defend the status quo are almost always threatened by any kind of change. They will often resist any effort to implement new ideas, even when those ideas are clearly derived from N.T. teaching.

If you are involved with such efforts to return to the N.T. ways and find yourself going against the grain, don't be intimidated. Keep in mind that your desire is not based on some kind of cultic fanaticism, but on biblical truth that has been articulated by a virtual consensus of N.T. scholarship, as demonstrated by Dunn's remarks.

Over the years I have met many saints with tremendous skills and talents.

Often, however, the 'church' they belong to has provided little opportunity to exercise these gifts. Instead, the 'powers-that-be' seem to dominate every aspect of church life while the role of all others has been limited to that of pew-sitters. Their only function is to passively absorb sermons and their only exercise is to pass the offering plate.

Does the church you belong to stimulate and cultivate your gifts and graces so that you can be a channel of blessing to others, or are you essentially passive, forced to keep your talents and insights to yourself?

Have you ever experienced the Lord's Supper in the setting of a shared meal, instead of something tacked on to the end of an 11 a.m. service? I can tell you from experience it is an edifying experience.

When are we going to stop leaving ministry to the "ordained" and see all of God's people as servants with significant ministries to carry out?

In Mark 7 some key observations can be isolated regarding detrimental traditions. Jesus' remarks about traditions are as relevant today as they were in the 1st Century.

1. The Pharisees were offended and puzzled when Jesus' disciples did not conform to their long-standing traditions, (v. 5).

2. These traditions originated from religious experts—"the tradition of the elders"—and had taken on the force of law over time.

3. Such traditions tend to multiply and become the focus of attention instead of more important issues, (v. 4; cf. Matt. 23:23-24).

4. When the worship of God is rooted in man-made rules it becomes vain (vv. 6-7). Hence the crucial importance of discerning what is of God and what is of man in our worship together.

5. When traditions are elevated as a standard, the commands of God take a backseat, (v. 8).

6. The commands of God will be flagrantly violated when zeal is directed towards observing traditions, (vv. 9-12).

7. The Word of God is made of no effect when people are fixated on traditions handed down from previous generations, (v. 13).

8. Fixation on traditions tends to permeate all of one's existence—"you do many things like that", (v. 13).

Given the effects deep-seated traditions have on people, it should not surprise us when others react defensively, heatedly, and even violently when their cherished assumptions are questioned. Jesus and His disciples faced the same kind of reactions in their ministries.

May the Lord Jesus give us boldness to speak the truth in love in these evil and confusing days. May the Lord give us humble spirits that are committed to other believers as commanded by apostolic tradition: "Let us consider how we may spur one another on toward love and good deeds; let us not give up meeting together, as some are in the habit of doing, but let us encourage one another—and all the more as you see the Day approaching" (Heb.10:24-25).

References:

1   *Baptist Reformation Review,* Summer 1981, pp. 31, 32

2.   Westminster Press, 1987, 156 pp.

3.   While in Durham, England, in 1986 I visited with Don Garlington, who was pursuing his Ph.D. under Dunn's supervision. I almost got to meet "Jimmy," as Don called him, but there was a note on his office door that he could not be disturbed because of his work on the Romans commentary.

4.   "The Lord's Supper in the Life of the Church." *Searching Together,* Autumn 1984, 32 pages.

5   *Unity and Diversity in the New Testament,* Westminster Press. 1977, p. 351

This article originally appeared in *Searching Together,* 20:1-3, 1992

CHAPTER 19
"WHO HAS THE AUTHORITY IN THE CHURCH?"

Norbert Ward

(Norbert was the founding editor of Baptist Reformation Review in 1972. Because of health issues, he asked Jon Zens to become the editor in 1978. Norbert died in 1980 in Nashville, Tennessee. What follows are excerpts from his lengthy article.)

STATEMENT OF THE PROBLEM

Russel T. Hitt demonstrates a problem of authority in the local church in the following statement:

> In one congregation an upper middle-class family found themselves in a conflict in their church because they bought a house that was not approved by their elder or "shepherd" (Russel T. Hitt, "The Soul Watchers," *Eternity*, April 1976, p. 14).

Mr. Hitt quotes the following from a seminarian's experience in a "Christian community" situation:

> The major principles I'm thinking of are what I called "charismatic guidance" (the belief that God gives guidance and direction to Christians without the necessary use of any external means, such as the Scriptures) and "submission," the belief that our Christian growth is best encouraged by submitting our wills to someone who is put over us in spiritual authority. During the year I was there the church developed problems as the two principles inevitably merged into one—that God would lead a Christian's spiritual life through the direct guidance of the person or persons in authority over him. Submission was exalted as the ruling principle of spiritual growth. In fact, the statement was often made, "it doesn't matter whether the guidance given

is right or wrong, God will bless you if you submit yourself to it regardless."
The kind of things that came up involved, for example, buying a certain
house and several dating situations (Hitt. p. 14).

We are in a day of exodus from the "establishment." This is as true in the church as it
is in the world. Thousands of little groups of "dissenters" are coming up all over the
world. We support those who continue to labor in the major denominations, but I
feel a real kinship with those who have separated.

The above quotes from Mr. Hitt's article show that the problem of authority is
not solved by separation from the "establishment" churches, but the problem often
becomes more serious. Reformed circles resist the concept that a "shepherd" is given
some sort of "charisma" to know what is best for the sheep in a matter without
Scriptural support, but there are many who hold the view that authority in the
church is by virtue of office and in the officers of the church alone. I would like
to call our attention to some basic principles of Christian life as individuals under
God, and Christian community (submitting ourselves one to another) under God.
I will argue against human authority as the central idea in any form of church life.

STRUGGLES WITH THE PROBLEM

My purpose is to try to show that there is a simple answer to the confusion and
controversy over the various issues of church government. I say that the answer is
simple, but I do not mean to say that the answer is easy. The answer is simple in that
there is *One* source of authority in the church. That authority (government) is in
the Lord Jesus Christ. Jesus said, "All power (authority) is given unto me in heaven
and in earth."

The answer, however, is not easy for several reasons. For one thing, we are in the
flesh. Even godly persons may seek the pre-eminence among the brethren. There is
little that pleases the natural man more than to have other people do what he tells
them to do.

It is not easy because we are often moved by prejudices. We often think that
because a thing has always been done in a certain way that this practice must certainly be the will of Christ in the church. We also may be prejudiced by the pressures
of the community. If the community (especially the religious community) expects a
church to do a certain thing, we may be moved to do the community's will, thinking
that it is God's will.

We often assume that authority is given to certain people within the church
and that to resist them is to resist God. However, we must not think that anyone
has within his own person the authority to direct the affairs of our lives without a
"thus says the Lord." Christ is the authority. We are all subject to His authority as
the Head of the church. The administration of the authority is in the hands of all
believers.

It is vital to the whole question of church life that we understand that every
believer has the same right to know the will of God. We must conclude, then, that

if a church is to know the will of Christ in her life, she must know the will of all the people.

Each believer is a priest and a king with Jesus Christ and has as much right to know the will of God in all matters as any other believer. If gifts differ from one believer to another, it follows that the influence of believers upon one another also differs. This difference in influence is supported by Scripture and is not just a logical conclusion. The church must, however, never forget the first principle of the priesthood of all believers. The church, then, can be most safely governed by the will of all the people, if the people's will is the will of God.

The church is not an ignorant nation or a business established for material gain. The church has one King, Jesus Christ, and those in the church are to pursue the will of the King.

THE AUTHORITY OF CHRIST IN THE CHURCH

As a first point in understanding the Lordship of Christ in the church, we should recognize that the church is His Body. In the existing decline and division of the church, it seems just too radical to think that the church is actually one body—the very body of Christ.

The Apostle Paul said, "And I, brethren, came not with superb speech or of wisdom, declaring to you the testimony of God. For I determined not to know anything among you, save Jesus Christ and him crucified" (1 Cor.2: 2). Paul describes his method as plain speech without sophistry. Paul was honest with his listeners and he did not deceive them with ideas of divinity within himself. He had a divine message. That message was Jesus Christ and Him crucified. Paul traveled as a messenger. He bore the testimony of God. Now, there lies the authority—"the testimony of God." "Jesus Christ and Him crucified" was Paul's message and the essence of his service.

The N.T. is clear that Christ is the head of the body. Christ is not an absentee landlord. He holds in His hands the means by which He directly executes His will within His body. Tradition, however, has held that He surrendered that authority to humans. This tradition I deny, and I believe that Paul established the doctrine of *one Lord* in the church. If Jesus has *all* authority, what is left for pastoral popes and Fundamentalist empire builders? I sometimes wonder if some traditional pastors delight in keeping the people in ignorance so that their dictatorship may continue. It seems that the term "mini-pope" is accurate in these situations.

The very word "ministry" should imply something to us. This word is used more often than any other in the N.T. to speak of those who serve the church. The word means the work or function of a *servant*.

I believe that a leader, pastor or otherwise, is very wrong and unfair to the consciences of other believers even to hint that he is being led by the Holy Spirit in any matter for which he cannot give a "thus said the Lord," and which is not validated by congregational approval. A claim of the leadership of the Holy Spirit is most often used to raise money. If a project is going to cost a good bit, the leader must have all the help he can get to convince the people to give to his pet project. So he must convince them that God is with him without a single word from God on the matter.

Is it not the case that many serious problems in local churches arise when either the leadership or part of the congregation comes to the conclusion that they have "the will of God" in a particular matter? Instead of taking this as a danger sign, indicating that the "will of God" for the church as a whole has not yet been found, a decision one way or another is ratified, thus "splitting" the body into camps. In some cases, of course, a parting of ways is unavoidable. But in many cases, I believe, the church could be held together if the brethren would wait longer, and seek the Lord together to see if they can reach unanimous agreement. Too often, we are not "swift to hear, slow to speak, and slow to wrath." Rather, we are moved to wrath, quick to speak (often in ignorance), and very slow to come and reason with our brothers and sisters.

This article originally appeared in *Baptist Reformation Review* (now *Searching Together*), 5:3, Autumn, 1976.

CHAPTER 20
UPON THE GROUND OF MEN?

Kat Huff and Jon Zens

All the versions of words that oppose other versions of words in Bible, the myriad of translations, gave me thought as to why this is happening, even today. A variant multitude of different Bible translations exist, each with their own name and individual trademark upon their version of the Bible. The reason for that is more than obvious to us. It is because of the many opinions of the various words that are used to express what each of the translation's authors "felt" or "thought" were most important or most accurate in their own understanding or their own interpretation, and were not "felt" to be in agreement or privy to other Bible versions. While we appreciate the effort that goes into each translation, the fact remains that they desired their own version in accordance to what they considered to be accurate in each of their minds.

THE BIBLE SAYS

We must appreciate the fact that most people are dependent on English translations, and pretty much assume that what they read is accurate. As Leland Ryken has pointed out:

> Readers who do not know the original biblical languages assume that an English translation reproduces what the Bible really says.... People naturally and legitimately appeal to the English translation in their hands as constituting "what the Bible says".... Readers of the English translation operate on the premise that they are reading what the Bible actually says (*The Word of God in English: Criteria for Excellence in Bible Translation,* Crossway Books, 2002, p. 136).

So then, may we be diligent in truth so that when we discover a bias, or a mindset, that has changed the meaning from the Greek word so that it then implicates something other than the intent of the original Author, should we not then perk up our ears to hear truth? Or should we be satisfied with an ear tickling from the opinions of the scribes according to the scribed version in which we agree? Do we just say, "Pick your favorite version, any version," and ignore the reality that not one of the multitude of versions are totally accurate?

May we seek the heart of our Father above the opinions of humans. When light is shed upon an inaccuracy or deflection from the Greek, may we have eyes to see and ears to hear Him. I have quite a few different versions myself, a whole entire shelf of them. And I'm thankful for them, but I also know that I need to seek Him as I read, and times do come when He points to a certain word or words, and so I then check out the Greek. Ultimately, He is our Teacher by the Spirit, just as He stated.

EXAMPLES OF PERSONALLY TRANSMITTED BIAS WRITTEN INTO TRANSLATIONS

The basic Greek word for "humanity" is *"anthropos."* This is a gender-inclusive word—it encompasses both men and women. In many translations, *"anthropos"* (singular) and *"anthropoi"* (plural) are translated as "man/men." Unfortunately, these renderings often do not lead to clarity, but contribute to confusion and mis-understanding. Here are some examples.

A PARTIAL SENTENCE OF PAUL'S CORRESPONDENCE LABELED AS EPHESIANS 4:8

"Therefore it says, When He ascended on high, He led captive a host of captives, And He gave gifts to *men*." (NASB)

The Greek Word

The Greek word here is *"anthropois,"* the plural form of *"anthropos."* It is not a gender-specific word.

Reality

"Therefore it says, "When He ascended on high, He led captive a host of captives, And He gave gifts to people."

The above mistranslation may not seem important, but let's remember that in his letter to the saints in Ephesus Paul writes concerning important gifts of function in the body of Christ—"apostles, and some as prophets, and some as evangelists, and some as pastors and teachers." (Ephesians 4:11) Are only males included in these functions? Phoebe was a deacon in the *ekklesia* in Cenchrae; Junia was an apostle (Romans 16:1, 7); Philip had four virgin daughters who were prophetesses (Acts 21:9).

A SENTENCE FROM PAUL'S CORRESPONDENCE LABELED AS 2 TIMOTHY 2:2

"The things which you have heard from me in the presence of many witnesses, entrust these to faithful *men* who will be able to teach others also." (NASB)

The Greek Word

The Greek word here is *"anthropois"* (plural), and it is an inclusive word that embraces men and women. Again, it is not a gender-specific word.

Reality

"The things which you have heard from me in the presence of many witnesses, entrust these to faithful people who will be able to teach others also."

A PARTIAL SENTENCE OF PETER'S CORRESPONDENCE LABELED AS 1 PETER 3:4

"But let it be the hidden *man* of the heart, in that which is not corruptible, even the ornament of a meek and quiet spirit, which is in the sight of God of great price." (KJV)

The Greek Word

The Greek word here is *"anthropos,"* which means this passage would more accurately read as "person." Again, it is not a gender-specific word.

Reality

"But let it be the hidden person of the heart, in that which is not corruptible, even the ornament of a meek and quiet spirit, which is in the sight of God of great price."

A PARTIAL SENTENCE OF PAUL'S CORRESPONDENCE LABELED AS EPHESIANS 3:16

"That He would grant you, according to the riches of His glory, to be strengthened with power through His Spirit in the inner man." (NASB version)

The Greek Word

The Greek word here is *"anthropon."* Again, it is not a gender-specific word.

Reality

"That He would grant you, according to the riches of His glory, to be strengthened with power through His Spirit in the inner person."

A SENTENCE OF PAUL'S CORRESPONDENCE LABELED AS 1 TIMOTHY 5:8

"But if any provide not for *'his'* own, and specially for those of *'his'* own house, *'he'* has denied the faith, and is worse than an infidel." (King James Version)

The Greek Word

In the context, Paul is speaking to women, specifically widows. The Greek phrase here is *"ei tis,"* which means "if anyone." Thus, even though females are being addressed, this translation of verse 8 has "his own," "his own house," and "he has denied."

Reality

"But if anyone does not provide for their own, especially those of their own household, they have denied the faith and are worse than an unbeliever."

A SENTENCE OF PAUL'S CORRESPONDENCE LABELED AS 1 CORINTHIANS 14:26

"What then, brothers? When you come together, each one has a hymn, a lesson, a revelation, a tongue, or an interpretation. Let all things be done for building up." (ESV)

The Greek Word

The Greek word here is *"adelphoi."* When *adelphoi* is used with reference to the body of Christ, it is always an inclusive word. Again, it is not gender-specific.

Reality

"What then, sisters and brothers? When you come together, each one has a hymn, a teaching, a revelation, a tongue, or an interpretation. Let all things be done for building up.

UPON THE GROUND OF MEN?

"Men are God's method. The church is looking for better methods; God is looking for better men. What the church needs today is not more machinery or better, not new organizations or more and novel methods, but *men* who the Holy Spirit can use—*men* of prayer, *men* mighty in prayer. The Holy Spirit does not come on machinery but on *men*. He does not anoint plans, but *men*—*men* of prayer." (E. M. Bounds)

I'm not implying for a second that E. M. Bounds was intentionally excluding parts of the body of Christ. It is just that when the gender-specific word is used, all else follows that same gender-divide. Even those who have a powerful revelation of Christ can communicate in a biased expression merely because of the wrongly translated words that are throughout the many versions of the Bible. Even when there is no intentional exclusion by the speaker or writer, the bias and wrongly translated non-gender words of the Bible versions dictate that such biased expressions become the norm. It becomes a common way of speech, because those are the words we read, over and over again, in the versions of the N.T. Writings. And usually no thought is ever given to the actual divisive implications for the body of Christ.

THE EVERYDAY REALITY OF OUR LIVES

Now, if you are thinking that it doesn't matter, because women always consider themselves to be included in that word, that the word "men" means both sexes in our minds and hearts, I think the reality of our lives shows the opposite.

For only two examples, I ask you the following questions: Do you, dear sister, open a door labeled "Men"? Or do you, dear brother, open a door labeled "Women"? Do you, my sister, generally shop for all your clothing needs in a store area labeled "Men"? Or do you, my brother, generally shop for all your clothing needs in a store area labeled "Women"? If you do, then never mind about this Greek word that is inclusive to both genders. However, if you do not, then imagine what else hides in the recesses of our perceived reality when we are exposed to such biased translations in the many Bible versions. This gender distinction has entered every facet of our lives together, it has deeply and subconsciously planted a bias into our minds, and we have accepted it as the reality of Christ. The implications are devastating and far-reaching, corrupting even the foundation of our everyday Life. Is it any wonder that the majority of the church has followed this biased mindset of unreality in its form?

THE WALLS OF THE WORLD

There is a great barrier created when we use these gender-biased words that are not accurate in accordance to the original inspired words, nor the mind of Christ. In the West, this barrier may appear as a mere vague shadow of difference, but this gender divide has become a hidden thought that plays out in the reality of our everyday lives together. We can only see the results of this gender divide if we step back and see with new eyes. And behold, there it is! Can you see it? It's everywhere. It is here among us. It's in the words we speak. It's in the things we do. It's in the way we raise our children. It's in the reasoning of our thoughts, and it's in the sight of our view.

We have become accustomed to this bias of gender distinction, and we accept it all the time without realizing it, because we no longer see the wall dividing us. We have been blinded to the secret power of the way of the darkness of this world. Thus, we cannot see that the wall is built from the perspective of the unbelieving world. This bias has no ground in Christ. He broke all the barriers, all the walls came tumbling down, and by Christ in us we are whole and complete. In Christ there is no divide, no walls, no hills, no valleys, but level ground. Even in the so-called "good" that we sometimes do, such as when we bring attention to the gender or race of other saints in appreciation for their expression of Christ, is misguided. The intent is to free and honor others, but in actuality, this is building upon the wall that divides us. Our Ground is level, all other ground is faulty, and will be shaken till it is level or no longer exists.

THE ONE NEW HUMAN

Paul's correspondence labeled as Ephesians 2:14-16 reads, "For He Himself is our peace, who made both groups into one and broke down the dividing wall of the barrier, by abolishing in His flesh the enmity, which is the Law of commandments contained in ordinances, so that in Himself He might create the two into one new man, thus establishing peace, and might reconcile them both in one body to God through the cross, by it having put to death the enmity," (NASB). The word translated here as "man" is the Greek word *"anthropon."* Yet again, it is not a gendered word of the flesh. This Greek word is more accurately translated as "human" or "person."

Reality, "so that in Himself He might create the two into one new human."

When the above Greek word is translated without bias, far more meaning is given to Paul's words in his writing to the saints in Galatia—"There is neither Jew nor Gentile, neither slave nor free, nor is there male and female, for you are all one in Christ Jesus," (Gal. 3:28, NIV).

And keep in mind that women were portrayed in the worst ways and functionally eliminated from church life in the period 250 – 1600AD. The only version of the Bible available from 400 – 1400AD was the Latin Vulgate, translated by Jerome, who was no friend to females. A few early church fathers even suggested that when women experience salvation in Christ, they are then made complete by becoming male (Joy Bussert, *Battered Women,* LCA, 1986, p. 9). So the idea that in Christ women really had an "inner man" was not far from the truth, as they saw it.

OUR UNSHAKEABLE GROUND

If there is any hope for the *ekklesia* (church) on earth today, it must begin with the foundation of everyday Life in our homes, in our families, so that when we as families come together as one family in Christ, we will know the reality of the fact that we are all priests in equal standing in the freedom that we have been given in Christ. I see no other alternative but to stand upon the one unshakeable Ground everyday of our shared Life. Christ Jesus is to be our only Ground, at all times, upon which we stand together as God's people. We cannot stand upon fallow ground and not falter when all other ground than Christ is being shaken and burned.

"IT'S A MAN'S WORLD"

We need to understand that there are women all over the world who deeply resent men, because of how men have taken advantage of them and sinned against them. In many parts of the world, women live in the cruel bondage of ownership by men. Thus, when they come to the Bible and see verses like, "For the grace of God that brings salvation has appeared to all men," and "God commands all men everywhere to repent," they figure the Scriptures are for men not for them. Most women in the world are taught to think that it is an advantage to be male and a minus to be born female. You can suggest that when women see the word *"men"* in Scripture, they see themselves included in it. But the truth is, to use the word *"men"* (in generic contexts) in the Bible is unnecessary and extremely misleading. The inspired reality of the translated Greek words would be best served with designations like "people," "humans," "men and women," "persons," "folks," and "brothers and sisters."

In our day, Zondervan's TNIV *(Today's New International Version)* probably does the best job of a solid translation which uses gender-inclusive words that more accurately reflect the original inspired Greek words rather than *"man/men."* For example, the TNIV in Ephesians 4:8 has, "when he ascended on high, he led captives in his train and gave gifts to his people."

(A storm of controversy surrounded the release of the TNIV in 2002. Ann Nyland has documented how certain evangelical leaders have tried to control what Bible versions are published in *More Than Meets the Eye: The Campaign to Control Gender Translation in Bibles* (2004). When a revision of the NIV was released in 2011, then Zondervan discontinued Bibles containing the TNIV. See Christian Examiner, http://www.christianexaminer.com/Articles/Articles%20Sep09/Art_Sep09_20.html for further information).

The image of God is both male and female (Genesis 5:2). In order for Christ to be expressed in His fullness, the manifestation of the Spirit in each part of the *"new humanity"* must be living and active. As God's people, may we be aware of any divisive bias that has influenced our thinking, so that together we may have the mind of Christ, and be found standing upon the one unshakeable Ground.

For Further Reflection:

Laurie Fasullo, "What about the word *Kephale* ('head') in the New Testament?" at www.searchingtogether.org/kephale.htm

Frank Viola, *"God's View of A Woman,"* at frankviola.org/2012/01/30/godsviewofawoman/

Jon Zens, *What's With Paul & Women? Unlocking the Cultural Background to 1 Timothy 2*

CHAPTER 21
HEALING FROM CHRIST FOR THE NATIONS

Stephen Crosby

The will to power is in all humanity. It's as old as the garden. It doesn't get any more primal in power than "you shall be as gods." That's the power statement of all power statements. Lord Acton's axiom about power tending to corrupt and absolute power corrupting absolutely, is not far off the mark. Our civil forefathers understood the need to restrain power. The appropriated and experiential Cross of Christ is supposed to address that issue for believers. Death precedes life. Strength and weakness, and suffering and glory co-exist side by side. A prevailing ethos of power is not helpful, but rather detrimental to a faith community that is trying to touch God in faith for healing. A culture of power is a culture of spiritual imperialism where life is framed in terms of victors and losers, be it in theological debate, interpersonal relationship, or engaging the issue of health and healing. We want disease and sickness to be on the loser side of the scale. However, a Christian's victory is not based on brute force, even in dominion over disease. It's based on death and resurrection. We must never lose sight of this.

Problems occur when we move from Calvary-based ministry to power-based efforts. This jeopardy is nowhere more serious than in the matter of the gifts of healings. There's a common three-fold categorization of the charismatic gifts. Allegedly, the three categories are: power, utterance, and revelation. Who says so? These are man-made prejudgments and categorizations. Who says healing is a power gift? Manifested power is the fruit of abundant faith and love. We want the gifts of healings to operate in our midst without the cost associated with maintaining personal relationships and identifying with the sufferer. We want to maintain our cultural value systems and still have power "on-tap" to make things happen, when we chant the name of Jesus. The kingdom doesn't work that way.

To effectively minister the gifts of healings you have to let yourself be touched by suffering. If you cannot weep privately, then you'll have no authority publicly.

Christ was a high priest touched by the feelings of our infirmities. Our culture keeps us busy and in a state of spiritual apathy and indifference, yet we expect God's power to flow on demand in our corporate gatherings. It will never happen in an expansive way in that kind of scenario. If we expect healings to flow, it means we must get engaged in the lives of others. Charles Péguy wryfully said this about Christians: Their hands are clean, but they have no hands. He was referring to the tendency in Christians to admire personal holiness and never be engaged with another human being in a meaningful way (cited in Paul Tournier, *The Whole Person in a Broken World*, New York: Harper & Row, 1964, p. 160).

This is painfully true in our attitudes, theology and methodologies of healing. We must invest our resources of time, money, energy, and emotions in others. Because of the prosperity of our culture, we think we can throw money at problems and make them go away. We pay professionals—doctors, lawyers, and preachers—to deal with our problems and make them go away. We're unwilling to divest ourselves of our right to our most precious resource: time. If healing is going to expansively flow in a believing community (and outside it) we will have to forgo our right to our time, energy, and emotions. Calvary claims them all.

I'm not talking about being burned up and used up in church activities. Part of being a good steward, as I have said, is saying "no" to things. I am talking about making time to touch others in need, whatever that might look like in local circumstances. I'm talking about being functionally led by the Spirit and adapting and changing whatever it takes in our lifestyle to make it happen.

When we don't see healings like we should, we can be disappointed, depressed, or downcast. Often this is because power hasn't been exercised for all to see and admire, not because of any deep point of identification with the needs of the physically oppressed. We're more concerned about how our prayer is going to make us look than if the sick are healed. We want to accrue power, and get a sense of value from power.

It is not God's fault that we're not healed. Five hundred trips through a prayer line, to be prayed over by individuals who are wittingly or unwittingly complicit with the devil in resisting the Cross of Christ, will not release healing. All of our spiritual activity can never fix a basic refusal to embrace the Cross; which is the divinely prescribed instrument of healing for that situation.

While the gifts of healings are not necessarily defined in terms of power, power is the result of their release. Healings are a war against death and disease and represent the ultimate power struggle. This is heady air to breathe. Many mighty ones have fallen victim to the intoxicating effects of having authority over disease. Even though power so easily corrupts, the Church must have an answer for the overt power grab that is occurring in our day by those secular forces that would have us dependent on them for our very lives. The Church needs to have an answer, not fighting fire with fire, matching strength for strength, but an answer according to Christ in resurrection and in the power of Calvary.

Power has been defined differently throughout our nation's history and culture. A generation ago it was defined by the equation: military + industry = power

= control. That's no longer true in modern Western societies. Today's power equation reads: information + capital = power = control. There is an emerging power structure that has the potential to control our very existence by creating physical dependency upon it. That formula is: medicine + money = power = control. More specifically it works out to be: pharmaceuticals + healthcare + government + money = power = control.

Because of the collusive elements of the above equations, and the skyrocketing cost of medical care and insurance premiums, there are literally millions of people who cannot afford to be sick. The choice for these is either complete financial ruin or dependency on the state. The day is coming for many believers when the options will be to experientially know Him as Healer, to sell our soul to the gods of this age, or to die. The whole matter of the gifts of the Spirit will move from the fringes of Sunday morning enthusiasms into life and death realities. A Church absorbed in Jesus Christ simply must arise. Not a Church strong in principles of organizational management and hierarchy, trying to outdo mammon in mammon's game, but rather a Church which looks only to Christ for triumph over disease. It simply must happen. Just as the Lord used persecution to push the believers out of Jerusalem, so the Church in our age is going to find itself similarly motivated from circumstantial necessities rather than enthusiasm and glitz in the days ahead.

Excerpts from: *Healing: Hope or Hype?* by Stephen Crosby. Eloquent Books: New York, 2009. Available in hard cover, soft cover, PDF, or Kindle/E-book at www.stevecrosby.com. Used with permission from the author.

CHAPTER 22

"THEY WILL LAY THEIR FREEDOM AT OUR FEET" (FROM: THE GRAND INQUISITOR)

Comments by Jon Zens

"The Grand Inquisitor"—a story Ivan tells Alyosha in the course of Fyodor Dostoyevsky's *The Brothers Karamazov*—contains some powerful images of past historical realities. They forcefully illustrate the shift from Jesus' teachings to raw political power in organized religion. The story focuses on the Roman Catholic Church. But the principles expressed can be applied in varying degrees to any religious group. There is a great warning in this story—a warning to obey Jesus' voice so as not to be squeezed into the world's mould (Rom. 12:1-2).

Ivan's story takes place in 16th Century Seville, Spain. The story springs from the poetic custom of those days to bring the heavenly powers down to earth. In Ivan's poem, Christ appears before a Cardinal (The Grand Inquisitor), but He says nothing—the Cardinal reveals much as he does all the talking. This was sort of a "coming" of Christ fifteen centuries after His death, resurrection, and promise to return.

At the peak of the Inquisition, Christ appears in Seville, when just the day before one hundred "heretics" had been burned "for the glory of God." The people recognize Him and are irresistibly drawn to Him. A blind man is healed and a seven-year old child is raised from the dead.

As the momentum toward Christ is gaining, the Cardinal appears. Angered by the good deed done to the child, he summons his "holy guard" to arrest Christ. In an instant, the masses forget about Christ and bow down to the earth before the old Inquisitor.

Christ is taken to a dingy prison. That night, the prison door opens and the Inquisitor comes in alone and shuts the door behind him. The Cardinal then embarks on a lengthy monologue in which he speaks openly of what he has thought in silence for ninety years. His speech provides us with much to think about.

The Cardinal is obviously disturbed by Christ's presence, and asks. "Why are You come to hinder us?" "Tomorrow I will condemn You and burn You at the stake as the worst heretic," he threatens.

The Cardinal points out that the key issue between *them* and *Him* is *freedom.* Christ promised freedom to men, but the Inquisitor is sure that "people are more persuaded than ever that they have a perfect freedom, yet they have brought their freedom to us and laid it humbly at our feet." An oft repeated theme in religion: *keep people in bondage in the name of freedom.*

The Cardinal sees no need for Christ to come back, for Catholicism will complete His work. The Cardinal is happy that Christ turned His work over to "the Church" so that she can bind and unbind. Thus Christ cannot think of taking away this authority. Hence the question, "Why have You come to hinder us?"

Can we not with propriety ask, *if Christ were to come now and visit all that goes on in His name, would He be met with the same question from 'Christian' leaders of all stripes,* "Why have You come to hinder our Agendas, Majorities, Denominations, Programs, Associations, Conventions, etc.?" Think about the implications of this reality.

The Cardinal then elaborates on just why Christ is such a hindrance to the system. It all boils down to three issues, which confronted Christ in the Temptation (Matt. 4:1-11). In these three issues—*miracle, mystery, and authority*— "the whole subsequent history of mankind is, as it were, brought together into one whole." The Cardinal without hesitation admits that "the Church" has taken its cue from the "dread spirit" (Satan), and rejected the replies of Christ to the evil one.

Miracle: *"He finishes the building who feeds them."* The Inquisitor perceives that "nothing has ever been more insupportable for a man and a human society than freedom." He knows that with a miracle—turning stones into bread—"mankind will run after You like a flock of sheep...though forever trembling lest You withdraw Your hand and deny then Your bread." But Christ, he also knows, taught that freedom is worthless if obedience is bought with bread. Thus "the Church" can keep men in bondage in the name of providing for them. The Cardinal chides Christ for rejecting "the one infallible banner which was offered to You to make all men bow down to You alone—the banner of earthly bread."

"You," the Cardinal observes, "did desire man's free love, that he should follow You freely, enticed and taken captive by You...having only Your image before him as his guide."

Is it not true that much of what goes on in the name of Christianity is not satisfied with *faith,* and therefore seeks to hold consciences captive by giving them something *tangible?* The Cardinal knew that men seek the miraculous, not God.

The Mystery: The Inquisitor mocks Christ for having a small flock, the elect, while "the Church" holds the masses with its visible signs. "If You came to the elect and for the elect," the Cardinal notes, "then that is a mystery and we cannot understand it." He continues, "if it is a mystery, then we too have a right to preach a mystery—a mystery which the faithful must follow blindly, even against their conscience." And what is "the Church's" mystery? *We are not working with You, but with him—the one who tempted You. That is our mystery."*

Authority: The Cardinal boasts, "we took from him, the wise and the mighty spirit of the wilderness, what You rejected with scorn—Rome and the sword of Caesar." The inquisitor was fully aware that in taking the sword "the Church" had rejected Christ and followed *him*. But such power "keeps the consciences" of men, and creates/sustains a unified whole.

Thus "the Church" must continually "persuade the people that they will only become free when they renounce their freedom to us, and submit to us." In order to accomplish this, the masses must be belittled—"we will show them that they are weak, that they are pitiful children, vicious, worthless and rebellious." At bottom, *they must be kept dependent like babies.*

In all of this, "the Church" will provide all the answers for their "cases of conscience," and the Cardinal is sure "they will be glad to receive our answer, for it will save them from the great fear and terrible agony they endure at present in making a free decision for themselves."

The Cardinal confesses that he once prized the freedom Christ gave, but "awakened, turned back and joined the ranks of those *who have corrected Your work.*" "I repeat, tomorrow You will see that obedient flock who at a sign from me will hasten to heap up the hot cinders about the pile on which I shall burn You for coming to hinder us. For if anyone has ever deserved our fires, it is You."

Jesus said nothing to the Inquisitor, but "the old man longed for Him to say something, however bitter and terrible." Christ arose suddenly in silence, and softly kissed the Cardinal on the forehead. That was His answer. The Inquisitor opened the prison door, told Christ to *never* come again, and let Him out into the dark alleys of the town.

So ends Ivan's story, and so begins our thought. Four things strike me. One, how "Christian" groups can side with him and dominate others, all in Christ's name. Two, how church leaders can be afraid of "freedom" among God's people, and therefore invent many ways to "keep them in line." Three, how people easily give in to the pressure to trade their freedom in for bondage—all in the name of freedom!

Fourth, how quickly we forget just what Jesus rejected in the Temptation.

Henry C. Vedder's generalizations seem appropriate at this point:

And so we are brought face-to-face with one of the greatest anomalies in history: *the religion of peace and righteousness and universal brotherhood becomes in a single generation the pillar of despotism and the foe of liberty, the apologist for every wickedness that may entrench itself in high places.* The Church has, on the whole, kept its part of the shameful contract better than the State. It surrendered to the world and devoted itself to the task of justifying the world's life—a life that in every act and principle in absolute negation of the teaching of Jesus.... There is little injustice or exaggeration in Tolstoy's summary:

The Church so transformed Christ's teaching to suit the world that there no longer resulted from it any demands, and that men could go on living as they had hitherto lived. The Church yielded to the world, and having yielded, followed it.... (*Socialism & the Ethics of Jesus,* Macmillan, 1912, 466-467).

This article originally appeared in *Searching Together,* 13:1, Spring, 1984.

CHAPTER 23
WHEN HAS AUTHORITY GONE TOO FAR?

Jon Zens

Jesus Christ rules His assemblies by the Spirit through His Word. Congregations have authority to carry out kingdom affairs in line with Christ's Word. The common notion that authority belongs only to a *segment* of the church (the "pastor," "the session," the "board," etc.) and not to the assembly *as a whole* cannot be sustained by the N.T.

It is from this misconception that wrong ideas of authority flow freely. Several propositions will follow that seek to summarize crucial matters regarding authority in the church:

1. *Any assembly of believers has authority to act on Christ's Word,* (Matt. 18:15-18; 1 Cor. 5:1-13; 6:1-8). If reconciliation does not take place at the lowest levels, offenses must be brought "to the assembly." The elders are certainly a part of that process, but they are not the process itself. The idea that "take it to the assembly" means "take it to the elders," as Jay Adams suggests, is not based in the N.T.[1] In 1 Corinthians 5 Paul does not chide the elders for not taking action, but instead confronts the whole assembly. In 1 Corinthians 6 Paul assumes that the brethren have the ability to work out their internal problems.

2. *Elders recognized by the people are responsible to equip the flock for ministry, to lead them into maturity, to teach and apply the Word. Elders are accountable to God for their oversight, and are to exercise their care of the flock in line with the servant-pattern of Christ,* (Acts 20:28; Heb. 13:17; Eph. 4:11-12; 1 Thess. 5:12; 1 Pet. 5:1-3).

3. *A mammoth problem exists because traditionally the "office of pastor" has been separated from the "elders," and given an authority unknown in the*

NT. "The Minister" concept has no denominational barriers—it is everywhere assumed. "The pastor" doctrine presupposes and perpetuates the clergy/laity distinction. In 1904, I.M. Haldeman asserted that, "Bishop and Elders do not exist today.... The Pastor is a Gift to the Church."[2] The Puritans believed that "a minister's authority derives from his office.... None can preach with authority but 'who is in office.'"[3]

This "office" is totally different from just being an "elder."[4] It has a "call" that other elders apparently do not receive. It has training (seminary, Bible school) not required of elders. Men sometimes leave their families for such training.[5] When they "enter the ministry," they become "the leading officer of a congregation."[6] As long as we assume that "the pastor" fits the job description given by David McKenna, problems of authority are inevitable.

[The pastor is] like the cerebellum, the center for communicating messages, coordinating functions, and conducting responses between the head and body....The pastor is not only the authoritative communicator of the truth from the Head of the Body, but he is also the accurate communicator of the needs of the Body to the Head...he edifies the Body.[7]

These words suggest that the pastor is a mediator between the Lord and His people. Christ nowhere assigns such tasks to one person. The fact that we think He does is the source of many problems.

4. *Perverted authority is often subtle, but Christ's sheep are able to sense its tentacles.* If a church atmosphere causes people to walk around with a dark cloud hovering over their heads (no joy, Gal. 4:15), to feel like they are being "watched" and "kept track of," and to feel like they can't act without "checking in" with the leadership, there is probably an authority problem.

SOME MARKS OF PERVERTED AUTHORITY INCLUDE:

1. The claim of direct authority from God which bypasses the need to test all things.
2. The command to "submit to me" replaces "I will serve you."
3. The method of leadership is to "order" people around instead of appealing to them to do the right things.
4. There is a dominating, "pushy" spirit instead of a dependence on the Lord to direct.
5. There is a sense of control instead of a sense of support.
6. A gift is exploited so that others are made to feel dependent on it
7. There is an inflexibility—"don't question me"—"don't touch the Lord's anointed."

8. There is inapproachability and intimidation—the "aura" around the leader keeps people in awe.

9. An organization emerges built upon a person and his peculiar emphases instead of around Christ and His Word.

10. There will be cyclical challenges to the authority figure (which are immediately and forcefully purged).

11. There is more concern for maintaining the authoritarian structure than there is for caring about the people.[8]

As you reflect on your own experience, it is apparent that what we call "cults" do not have a monopoly on these tragic attributes. They too often permeate the structures of "Christian" groups and churches.

Notes:

1. *Ready to Restore,* Pres. & Ref., 1981, pp. 3-4

2. *How to Study the Bible,* Revell, 1904, pp. 395-396

3. "The Puritan View of the Ministry," *Banner of Truth,* Aug., 1957, pp. 29-30

4. "Elders," Charles Whitworth, *Reformation Today,* March-April, 1983, p. 13

5. "When Rev.—left his home [in Africa] to attend—Seminary, his wife was expecting their tenth child. The child was born four months after he left, but died a few days later. The loss brought great sorrow to—, but did not lessen his determination to make the sacrifices necessary to gain a strong training in biblical theology" (from a seminary bulletin).

6. *Covenanter Witness,* Aug. 30, 1972, p. 6

7. "The Ministry's Gordian Knot," *Leadership,* Winter, 1980, pp. 50-51

8. I am indebted to Mark Sequeira for this excellent summary

This article originally appeared in *Searching Together,* 13:1, Spring, 1984

CHAPTER 24
BRITICISMS IN THE UNITED STATES: "REVEREND"

H.L. Mencken

The Protestant Episcopal Church, on account of its affiliation with the Church of England and its generally fashionable character, is a distributing-station for Anglo mania in the United States, but its influence upon the language seems to be slight.... The fashionable preparatory schools for boys, most of which are under Protestant Episcopal control, have introduced a number of Briticisms into the vocabulary of their art and mystery.... At Groton, the most swagger of all the American prep-schools...the *staff* is actually called the *faculty,* and the *headmaster,* a Protestant Episcopal clergyman, is listed as *Rev.,* with the *the....*

I have spoken of the American custom of dropping the definite article before *Hon*(orable). It extends to *Rev.* and the like, and has the authority of very respectable usage behind it. The opening sentence of the *Congressional Record* is always: "The Chaplain, *Rev.* —D.D., offered the following prayer".... I also find the honorific without the article in the New International Encyclopedia, (and) in a widely popular American grammar-book.

The Episcopalians in the United States, at least those of the High Church variety, usually insert the *the* but the rest of the Protestants omit it.... Now and then some evangelical purist tries to induce the Methodists and Baptists to adopt *the* Rev., but always in vain. Throughout rural America it is common to address an ecclesiastic *viva voce* as *Reverend.* This custom is also denounced by the more delicate clergy, but equally without effect upon the prevailing speech habit. Some years ago one of the suffering brethren was thus moved to protest in verse:

> Call me *brother* if you will;
> Call me *Parson*—better still.
> Or if, perchance, the Catholic frill

Doth your heart with longing fill—
Though plain *Mister* fills the bill,
Then even *Father* brings no chill
Of hurt or rancor or ill-will.

To no D.D. do I pretend,
Though *Doctor* doth some honor lend,
Preacher, Pastor, Rector, Friend,
Titles almost without end
Never grate and ne'er offend;
A loving ear to all I bend
But how the man my heart doth rend,
Who blithely calls me *Reverend!*

When it came into use in England, in the 17th Century, *Rev.* was commonly written without the article, and immediately preceding the surname. Thus, Bishop Joseph Hall (1574-1656) did not hesitate to write *Reverend Calvin.* But at the beginning of the 18th Century the and the given-name began to be added, and by the end of the century that form was almost universal in England....

Dr. S.E. Morrison tells me that the Mathers were probably the first American divines to call themselves *Rev.* Increase Mather seems to have picked up the title during his visit to England, 1688-92. Before that time American clergymen were simply *Mr.,* and abbreviation of *Master.* This was an indication that they were masters of arts... There were relatively few *Doctors of Divinity* in America before 19th Century. The degree was seldom given by American universities. But any clergyman who has published an edifying work could obtain it from one of the Scottish universities on payment of a fee, and in the middle of the 18th Century, it was not unusual for an admiring congregation to pass the hat to help its shepherd obtain the degree.

In the list of members printed in the first tract of the Society for Pure English (1919) *Rev., Very Rev., Hon.,* and *Rt. Hon.,* appeared without the *"the"* and it is commonly omitted by the English Methodists and Baptists....

In general, ecclesiastical titles are dealt with somewhat loosely in the United States. In England an archbishop of the Established Church is the *Most Rev.* and *His Grace,* and a bishop is *the Right Rev.,* and *His Lordship....* Among Catholics, by the prevailing interpretation of a decree of the Sacred Congregation of Rites (1930), an archbishop who is not a cardinal is now *the Most Rev.* and *His Excellency (Excellentia Reverendissima),* and so is a bishop...a cardinal, of course, remains *His Eminence....*

The American bishops and archbishops display a dubious Latinity by their assumption of *the Most Rev. Reverendissimus,* to be sure, is a superlative, but in the situation in which it is used Latin superlatives are understood only in the sense of very, e.g., *altissimus mons* means a very high mountain, not the highest mountain. Moreover, if the bishops and the archbishops are entitled to be called *the Most Rev.,* and then so are the monsignori, for Rome applies reverendissimus to all of them alike....

The use of *Reverend* as a vocative (usually pronounced *revrun*) with no name or title following it, seems to be American. The DAE does not list this form, but it goes back to 1877 at least, for in that year Mark Twain used it. It has been denounced frequently, usually on the ground that *reverend* is an adjective, but Ehrensperger argues that this objection is not valid....

Not a few clergymen, revolting against being addressed as *Reverend*, and lacking the dignity of a *divinitatis doctor* (D.D.), have tried to induce their patients to call them *Mr.*, but not often with success, for many Americans have a feeling that Mr. Is rather too worldly and familiar for use in addressing a man of God. The Catholics get around the difficulty by using Father, and the High Church Episcopalians imitate them. In the South, *Reverend* is used in addressing colored clergymen for the purpose of avoiding calling them *Mr.* The Style Manual of the Department of State bans it, and also insists that the precedes Rev....

(The Style Manual) devotes nine pages to ecclesiastical titles, followed by a blank page for further notes. It begins with the Pope and runs down to the superiors of Catholic and Episcopal brotherhoods. There is no informal style, it says, for addressing the Pope: he is always *His Holiness the Pope* or *His Holiness Pius XI* on the envelope of a letter, and Your Holiness in the salutation thereof....

A Mormon bishop, as the Style Book notes, has no ecclesiastical title at all: he is plain Mr.... The Style Book is vague about the proper form of address to the superior of a Catholic sisterhood: she may be, it says, either the Reverend Mother Superior, Mother Superior, or Sister Superior, according to the rules of her order....

The Style Manual of the Dept. of State clings to the doctrine that Mr. Is good enough to be put on an envelope addressed to an ordinary American....

In the South the question whether members of the Negro race should or should not be accorded the ordinary American honorifics constantly agitates publicists. When, in 1940, the colored teachers of the Durham (N.C.) public school received notices of reappointment bearing *Miss, Mrs.,* or *Mr.* before their names there was loud rejoicing in Aframerica. It seemed, indeed, to be almost too good to be true....

In an article in *Ken* in 1939, R.E. Wolseley told the sad story of a young Northern journalist who went to the South and began describing blackamoors in a paper of the Bible Belt as *Mr., Mrs.,* and *Miss.* When protests poured in from local guardians of the Caucasian hegemony he sought for light and leading in his paper's Southern exchanges. Said Mr. Wolseley:

He found out that some eight or ten devices have been invented by Southern journalists to avoid using *Mr., Mrs.,* and *Miss* in front of the names of Negroes. They are: *Mademoiselle, Madame, Professor, Doctor, Reverend, Uncle,* and *Aunt.*

These excerpts are taken from *The American Language: An Inquiry into the Development of English in the United States.* (Alfred A. Knopf, 4th Ed., 1937), pp 268, 279, 280, 281, 283; and *The American Language: Supplement 1* (Alfred A. Knopf. 1966), pp 546, 547, 548, 555, 556.

CHAPTER 25

THE FULLNESS OF CHRIST: PERSPECTIVES ON MINISTRIES IN RENEWAL

John Howard Yoder

(What follows are excerpts from the above article which appeared in Concern #17, *February 1969, pp. 33-93. The whole article is excellent. Since it is no longer available, I have tried here to capture some of Yoder's key points, in order to highlight some foundational concerns. —Jon Zens)*

The following text is presented to provide a focus for conversation. The attempt is not made to carry on a conversation with the major alternative positions.

THE UNIVERSALITY OF THE RELIGIOUS SPECIALIST

There are few more reliable constants running through all human society than the special place every human community makes for the professional religionist. We may consult comparative religion, anthropology, sociology, or psychology…the report is always the same. Every society, every religion, even the pluralistic and "secular" civilization makes a place for the religionist. The basic cultural-anthropological parallel is all the more striking in view of a great variety of superficial differences.

    1. How this man becomes qualified may vary
        a. he may have received a special education or initiation
        b. he may have been born into a priestly family
        c. he may have been equipped by sacramental action
        d. he may demonstrate exceptional "charismatic" capacities
        e. he may be authorized by someone qualified to assign that status

But in every case he disposes of a unique quality, which he usually possesses for life, which alone qualifies him for his function, and besides which the mass of men are identified as "laymen", *i.e.,* non-bearers of this special quality. Normally one such person is needed per social group. One person per place is needed per social group.

2. The public performance identifying his office may vary
    a. In Catholicism he renews the miracle of the sacrament
    b. In magisterial Protestantism he proclaims the Word as true teaching
    c. In revivalism he moves his hearers to repentance and commitment
    d. In (Norman Vincent) Pealism he encourages people to be happy
    e. In suburbia he counsels them to be authentic

But in every case it is what only he can do right, and it is that function around which that happens which people think of as a "church."

3. It is, in fact, *his presence, which is the presence of the church;* he is the definition (sociologically) of the church...where the sacramental person is present. *Where he/she is absent, the church is not engaged.*

4. Despite the *outward appearance of his liturgical service* (2 above), what the *religionist's presence means to the individual and the society,* and the reason he is given his status, is perhaps more basically the "blessing" he brings to life....
    a. He may be encountered at the landmarks of the individual's life: puberty, (confirmation, baptism); marriage; parenthood; (baptism or "presentation"); death
    b. He may be expected to stand by especially in crisis and catastrophe: accident; sickness; drought or storm; war...

Whatever the mix of these various dimensions, in all of them the clergyman mediates between the common life and the realm of the "invisible" or the "spiritual"..., which one needs to lean on especially at those critical points of life.

5. No one balks at what his services cost

RELIGION IN THE OLD TESTAMENT:

The priesthood of Israel takes over most of the traits of the general religionist. The priest is qualified by heredity and initiation. He presides over celebrations of the annual cycle and blesses the king. In sum, in Israel the function of the religionist is present, accepted, used, but it is also filled with new meaning, relativized in value, and removed from the center.

THE VOCABULARY OF MINISTRY IN THE NEW TESTAMENT

If we come to the N.T. with this "professional religionist" view of ministry, asking, "What is said on this subject?" then we can add together some things which Paul said about himself as apostle, some things he wrote to Timothy and Titus about themselves, some other things he wrote to them about bishops and deacons, some things Acts reports about the leaders in Jerusalem and Antioch, salt the mixture with some reminiscences from the O.T., and come up with quite an impressive package as the "Biblical View of Ministry". But if we ask whether any of the N.T. literature makes the assumptions listed above:

1. Is there one particular office

2. In which there should be only one or a few individuals

3. For whom it provides a livelihood

4. Unique in character due to ordination

5. Central to the definition of the church

6. And the key to her functioning?

Then the answer from the biblical material is a resounding negation.

There is no concept (in the N.T.) of "laity" in the negatively defined sense, as "those with no ministry" (cf. G. Alan Richardson, *Introduction To Theology of the N.T.* p. 301). The people *(laos)* includes all the ministries. The bishop is a member of the laity just like everyone else.

THE MEANING OF MINISTRY IN THE N.T.

The most striking general trait is what we may call the *multiplicity* of the ministry. Under this label we gather three distinguishable observations:

1. The *diversity* of distinct ministries; that there are many, and the listing vary

2. *Plurality.* The fact that in some roles, notably the oversight of some congregations, several brethren together carried the same office

3. *The universality* of ministry: that "everyone has a gift" is said explicitly in 1 Corinthians 7:7, 12:7; Ephesians 4:7, and 1 Peter 4:10, and implicitly in Romans 12:1. Does this multiplicity have a theological meaning? The multiplicity of gifts assigned by the one Lord who fills all is thus itself an aspect of Christ's saving work and of His rule from on high.

The "fullness of Christ" in Ephesians 4:13, or the "whole body working properly" of Ephesians 4:16 is precisely the interrelation of the ministries of Ephesians 4:11, 12 in line with the divine unity of Ephesians 4:3-6. "Unity of the faith", "mature humanity", and "measure of the stature of the fullness of Christ" are not descriptions of a well-rounded Christian personality but of the divinely co-ordinated multiple ministry.

The conclusion is inescapable that the multiplicity of ministries is not a mere *adiaphoron,* a happenstance of only superficial significance, but a specific work of grace and a standard for the church.

The vestiges of the multiple ministry remained in the (theoretically) sevenfold ministry of the medieval church. Yet despite the persistence of these vestiges, the anthropological constant...soon wore off the originality, the universality of the first age. The special clerical class was soon there again, with the term "lay" redefined as "non-ministerial"...and Christianity had lost it's cutting edge.

Losing the specific and original trait of the primitive community, the church by and large became again subject to the usual anthropologically universal pattern of the single, sacramentally qualified religionist. By and large...this pattern has continued to our day in churches of every polity and theology.

RENEWAL EFFORTS:

It is a change, but not a fundamental one, when instead of serving a parish (the parish priest)...or withdrawing from society (the monastics), the clergy goes "out into the world". This began with the teaching orders (Jesuits, Dominicans).

It is another change, but again not a fundamental one, when churchmen use laymen to help with the church. The Reformers used statesmen, the princes in Luther's Germany and the city governments in Zwingli's Switzerland, to implement the Reformation when the bishops refused to do it.... Reformation proclamation of the priesthood of all and the right to read Scripture laid the groundwork for a different vision, but Reformation practice kept the church under the control of the statesmen and the university.

WELLHAUSEN'S CHILDREN

(The concept of multiple ministry) has not been one of the classic options in the inter-denominational arguments of the last four centuries.... Some of these are implicitly or explicitly arguments in favor of the abandonment of the multiplicity in favor of the mono-pastoral pattern, and to these we turn first.

It is one of the commonly held beliefs of N.T. scholarship in recent years that one can discern within the documents of the N.T. literature itself the signs of a marked evolution in patterns of ministry. In the young churches which arose directly out of the ministry of Paul, whose life we see reflected in his correspondence with them while they were still very young—for example, in the Corinthian letters—there was great spontaneity, even confusion, of enthusiasm and creativity, with a variety of "gifts" and "ministries" which to our tastes would appear to be chaotic. Paul did not deplore this enthusiasm (they say), but neither did he prescribe it.

In the Pastoral Epistles (they say), written much later, the picture changes. Here there is a bishop chosen according to certain prescribed criteria, exercising a defined function. Thus in the space of the time between these two sets of writing the apostolic church had already gone most of the way toward the "Early Catholicism" which made the bishop, by virtue of his office and independently of the congregation, the guarantor of apostolicity.... Many would apply this argument not to the ministerial question alone, but also to the larger questions of order and orderliness: *maturation means movement away from charismatic confusion to prescribed, routinized institutions,* and the church should not let a false spirituality frighten her away from such responsible sociological adulthood.

(However), if we do not posit a rigid uniformity of pattern in each age and do not distort interpretation by extrapolating backward from the next century, *nothing in the Pastorals negates the generally pluralistic structure we see elsewhere in the N.T.*

THE CENTRALITY OF PREACHING

Especially since the Reformation, the "proper preaching of the Word" has been central in definitions of both the church and her ministry. Just what the "Word" means and what the "proper" means have varied immensely from Luther to Calvin, and from Wesley to Barth, but formally the criterion has remained stable.

What we need to test here is not primarily whether the term "proclamation" is biblically derived, nor whether there should be "proclamation" in the church, but a much narrower question. Is the word's definition sufficiently objective and clear that anyone can use it and get the same "measurement"?

To move from the preachers of Acts to the teacher of James 3, or the teaching elder of the Pastorals, from Calvin to Finney to Billy Graham, and think one word covers that all, is simply to render that word useless.

Let us then ask first not whether there is a clear, solid concept of preaching, but whether there was in the N.T. one particular preaching office, identifiable as distinctly as the other ministries. The N.T does speak of a *kerygma* or proclamation.... But the corresponding personal pronoun *keryx,* preacher or herald, is used only three times, twice as a synonym for apostle (1 Tim. 2:7; 2 Tim. 1:11) and once for Noah. Many of the N.T. ministries involve verbal communications which can be conceived broadly as "proclaiming," but neither in the most varied picture (Corinthians) nor in the least varied (Pastoral Epistles) is there one particular ministry thus defined.

There were in the early church, and there are today, many kinds of verbal communication.... But the very effort to pull just one strand, one set of phrases or propositions, one way of speaking, or one audience, or one minister, as "central" to all others, has not yet yielded a solid yardstick, and has thereby refuted itself.

CONTEXT AND CONTENT IN NEW TESTAMENT PREACHING

Having sought in vain for a *particular* concept of preaching to serve as a criterion for church and ministry, let us keep the word as a general label for the varieties of verbal ministry in N.T. times.

Only by guess and surmise do we construct a notion of what the early church services were like... Apostles, elders, and teachers must all have preached in divers other ways, but without any hint that one kind of speech has priority. Yet there is one genuine distinction. C.H. Dodd has demonstrated that when speaking to non-Christians the early church did have a most specific message. Here the "proclamation" spoke of the life, death, and resurrection of Jesus, followed by a summons to repent and believe.

It is clearly possible to distinguish from this those teaching processes in the church which presuppose the listener's faith...it did make a difference to the N.T. preacher whether his listener was in the church or outside of it, a difference not only in tactics but in content.

Thus we have come upon a new dimension of definition, and a much more solid one—"proclamation" defined not by a specific office but by a specific listener, namely the unbeliever. But this is clearly not what the Reformation meant, for the whole concern of Reformation theology was to justify restructuring the organized church without shaking its foundations. The Reformation retained infant baptism and state-coerced church membership, thus the distinction between believers and unbelievers, members and non-members could not become visible. The true church had to be defined *independent of its membership.* "The church is where the word is properly preached and the sacraments properly administered" is a criterion applying to the *pastor* and the *synod,* not the *congregation* or the Christian.

MAGISTERIUM AND MAGISTRACY

George H. Williams has given currency to the term "magisterial" to define the official Reformation. It points to two different characteristics of the medieval and Reformation pattern: that the ministry was managed by the State (the magistracy) and that it was basically a theological teaching function whose standards were set in the universities (the magisterium). The inter-working of these two dimensions in the institution providing for one trained supported minister per parish continues to be the pattern by which it seems other approaches must be judged, even though its initial political backing by government has been abandoned by most societies.

No pattern of social leadership has been more fixed in the history of the race than that of the professional religionist. No pattern of ministry has been less flexible in Christian history than the placing of one priest or parson per parish.

We must therefore ask what, within the diversity of apostolic teaching and practice, are the constants, made all the more significant by their solidity in the context of change. Among these *constants within flexibility* would need to be included:

1. What we have called "multiplicity" in its various dimensions

2. Plurality: several persons with the same function, spiritually in the eldership

3. Diversity: many different identifiable roles

4. Universality: no one is not a minister

5. The constant need for the elder-bishop-pastor function of government in the local congregation

6. The constant need for the strategic teacher function maintaining the community's link with its past

At the same time we must seek responsibly for *principles of movement within the stability.* If we reject change, both for it's own sake and inflexibility, there must then be responsible tools of change.

1. The accredited prophet whose discomfiting urgings are not written off as unbalanced

2. The itinerant agent of relationship to the rest of the church, bearer of new and old ideas and questions

3. The servant of the Word, finding in Scripture hitherto unseen guidance

The above outline has intentionally centered on one-sided exposition of a thesis. The reason for this is simple; the current debate has not been marked by the presence of the option represented here, and therefore there are no current answers to it either....

"Having gifts that differ, according to that grace which was given us, let us use them according to the proportion of faith."

This article appeared in *Searching Together,* 11:3, Autumn, 1982.

CHAPTER 26
HOW ROMAN CATHOLIC ARE WE?

Jon Zens

The truth has nothing to be afraid of.

For years many non-Catholics have chuckled under their breath when hearing about *The Index of Forbidden Books* maintained by the Roman Catholic hierarchy. As of 1952 there were 4126 specific books that Catholics *could not* read, in addition to other general classes of forbidden books.

Redmond A. Burke—a Catholic librarian—wrote, *What is the Index?*, in 1952 (Bruce Pub., 129pp). This book intends to give "a clear and complete explanation of the Catholic position on reading." Burke's efforts provide us with a springboard to consider our own stance, and to ask ourselves: "How Roman Catholic are we in our perspective?" After reading *What Is The Index?* I'm convinced that there are pockets of immaturity equally rampant in "Protestantism." Non-Catholicism is filled with its own brand of "Indexes" too!

CHURCH CONTROL

Burke suggests that the Catholic Church "has had to extend a controlling hand" in what its adherents read because "the church is the custodian of divine revelation" (pp. 1, 3). Hence, the "whole structure" of the "Church's control of literature" rests upon an alleged God-given protective function of the church.

The practical effect of this outlook is that "truth" issues forth from only one visible institution. Everything outside of the prescribed boundaries is looked upon with suspicion. Are not a number of "Bible-believing" groups and denominations skilled at creating in their adherents a suspicion of sources outside of their orbit? Emotional catch-words—"Liberal," "Dispensational," "Calvinist," "Arminian," "Charismatic," "Antinomian," "legalistic"—are heaped upon those who veer from the party line.

Most of the time, "control" of what people associate with comes not so much out of the motive to preserve truth, but out of the necessity to preserve vested interests.

If people *think*, and acquaint themselves with various avenues of information, they may not remain in the institutions which allegedly possess the truth. Hence, adherents must be warned about the danger of contraband literature, etc.

AVOID RUIN

Burke says that the Catholic Church must "discourage the reading of those works endangering faith and morals" (p. 5). "Dangerous books" can "fall into the hands of others and possibly ruin their faith" (p. 69). Therefore, "the Catholic Church legislates to control error which corrupts the faith" (p. 34).

This view supposes that the truth needs props to hold it up. It also assumes that people will leave the truth unless it is enforced by outward influences. But truth will stand in the midst of any scrutiny or examination. Nothing can pull God's people away from truth—for Christ is the truth (John 14:6; 10:27-29).

Again, this legislative approach makes the adherents suspicious of all other groups but their own. They assume other outside sources must be avoided, unless the leadership approves of them.

The usual assumption is that non-Catholic works do contain doctrinal errors and may not be read until the contrary is proved by competent Catholic authorities (p.34).

How many Bible-believers are infected with an attitude that negatively prejudges any source outside their own tradition? Do they not often assume that they must stay away from other traditions unless the pastor, elders or denomination puts their stamp of approval on them?

"TRADITION" GETS THE SPOTLIGHT

The institutional watchdog perspective ends up defending past history instead of listening to Scripture. Burke cites the *Code of Canon Law* (1917) concerning the duties of "Censors of Books."

> These examiners, in discharging their office, should set aside all personal considerations and shall keep before their eyes only the dogmas of the Church and the universal doctrine contained in the Decrees of General Councils, in the constitutions and orders of the Holy See and in the consensus of approved doctors (Canon 1393).

The Bible is not mentioned as something to keep your eyes on. The driving force is tradition, not Scripture. How often has the "Presbyterian," "Baptist," or any other tradition been arduously defended with little serious examination of Scripture? Traditions have a habit of climbing up the ladder of our priorities. As a result, Christ is crowded out.

We must always remember, as Robert Brinsmead pointed out, that only Christ's history is without blemish. All other history stands under God's judgment. Our justification comes through Christ's holy history, not through the tarnished legends of a religious tradition.

When the institution—whether a local church or a large denomination—becomes uppermost, then "heresy" is defined as a departure from what the institution has declared in the past to be the "truth" (cf. Burke, p. 63).

"TRUST US"

In control-oriented religious groups, someone has to arbitrate what is acceptable and unacceptable. That "someone" is the leadership, be it singular or plural. Adherents are told to avoid other sources of information solely on the "authority" of the leaders. The Catholic hierarchy then, can "forbid books to their members for a good reason" (p.19).

When the leadership speaks, no explanation is necessary. The people are not encouraged to *think* things through, they are asked to uncritically *trust* their leaders. The problem often is, however, that in order for the leaders to maintain their domain, they must keep people from hearing/reading other sources. This is done in the name of "defending the purity of the faith," or "guarding the flock from error."

Hence, in Catholic libraries "forbidden books must be kept in a separate compartment apart from the open shelf collection" (p. 24).

STAY ON PROVEN PATHS

Burke points out that any notes in a Catholic version of the Bible need not be verbatim quotations from the Church Fathers and scholars, but must convey to the reader the traditional interpretation of the Scripture, (p. 29).

Since traditions are self-defending it is no wonder that "outside" sources that challenge or raise questions are labeled as "dangerous." Adherents are told to stick with the "safe" status quo of the past. That which raises questions and rocks the boat is viewed as a threat to the "unity" maintained by the bonds of tradition.

NO "PRIVATE" INTERPRETATION

Control-orientation creates a situation where people are spoon-fed and not encouraged to study on their own. In fact, people are made to feel guilty for wanting to study. They should just listen to those "competent"—the leadership. The banning of books is no violation of human liberty, since the Church is the "competent authority in religious matters and must therefore withdraw from circulation any books that may cause a breakdown of faith...private interpretation of the Bible has unfortunate results, (p. 48).

"Private interpretation," of course, means understanding that deviates from "the traditional interpretation of Scripture." Study of sources outside of the party-line boundaries can only lead to "heresy," since the institution claims to already have the "truth." Further study is unnecessary.

PUTTING HEDGES AROUND "TRUTH"

Inherent in the control-orientation position is the notion that truth in Christ is not sufficient to keep the allegiance of those who profess it. This view carries with it a tremendous fear that "error" can tear those who love Christ away from truth. Thus, possession of a forbidden book becomes a serious problem.

Those permitted to read forbidden books must carefully guard such volumes, perhaps the most effective manner being to place them under lock and key...priests and scholars permitted to read and keep forbidden books in their private libraries should provide for their proper disposition upon death. To neglect this important matter may cause scandal or endanger the spiritual welfare of others (p. 74).

But underneath the concern for "error's" power is really a fear that people will find something more satisfying than the party line.

SELF-RIGHTEOUSNESS FOSTERED

Human nature as it is, when people obey what the party line says, they pride themselves in what they have "separated" from. They have a false sense of "purity" because they have not touched the "unclean" thing. Burke points out that in order to encourage Catholics to read their version of the Bible:

Leo XIII in 1898 granted a special indulgence for those who would spend at least fifteen minutes a day in reading the Bible, and a plenary indulgence once a month for reading of the Bible.... Bible reading is regarded as something meritorious by the Catholic Church (p. 77).

While Protestants in theory recoil at the thought of human actions being "meritorious," many who are faithful to various party lines manifest a very self-righteous spirit. They act like God is more pleased with them because they are not "charismatic," "Calvinistic," "Dispensational," etc. Virtually every tradition looks down its nose in some way at those outside their ghetto.

TRUTH NEEDS LOVE, NOT PROPS

If a person has been truly drawn to Christ by the Spirit, then no error can pull him away from that commitment (Gal. 5:10; John 10:5, 27-30; Phil. 1:1; 1 John 4:4). Truth in Christ is not afraid of investigation. If what we believe/practice is according to truth, we have nothing to fear from questions that may be raised. If what we believe/practice is false, then we ought to welcome any source of correction.

Those who refuse to entertain questions, who will not enter into dialogue before an open Bible, who cast aspersions on "outsiders," who discourage the study of various viewpoints, and who refuse to gain possible help from a variety of viewpoints, and who refuse to gain possible help from a variety of sources, are probably defending something other than truth. If we have some measure of truth, why should we be defensive about it? Why should we feel threatened by challenges to our position?

A loving open atmosphere nurtures truth. If "truth" must be enforced by external forces then probably vested interests and tradition rather than truth are at stake. If people's commitment to "truth" must be gained and maintained by such things as fear, guilt, intimidation and suspicion of others, then it is doubtful that truth is really the issue in their lives.

THE RESPONSIBILITY OF ELDERS

Paul said, some are "to exhort in sound teaching and to refute those who contradict," (Titus 1:9). No doubt many church leaders are motivated by such passages as these when they warn the brethren about things/people "contrary to our tradition." However, there is a fine line between godly concern for the flock's relationships to Christ, and exerting control over people that seeks only to preserve the party line and to squelch legitimate inquiries. Why is that the "rule" of the elders is so often used as the basis for unquestioning obedience—"You must go along with this because the elders say so"? The degree that something threatens the party line will determine how much of the "authority" of certain people will be called upon to resolve the situation.

In the name of "truth," an elder reprimanded one young man for having a copy of *S. T.* in his Bible. He was told that if he read this magazine, he could no longer teach Sunday School in that church. In another church, the people were warned not to read a certain article in *S. T.* because it would confuse them. One brother told us that for several years he avoided *S. T.* because a pastor told him it was "dangerous." After reading it for himself, his opinion changed. These are a few examples I know of; you probably are aware of similar cases related to a variety of areas in church life. Is the truth or some party line usually at stake in such actions?

If something is from Christ, how can we be afraid of it? If something is erroneous, must we resort to innuendo, emotional phrases and unkind words to refute it?

Jesus Christ is the Truth (John 14:6). Paul always dealt with error as it affected people's relationship with Christ (Col. 2:1- 4, 17, 19). We do well to trust God's Spirit to lead His people into truth. We need to live in brokenness and humility, knowing that there is yet much that the Spirit will teach us. In the historical process, truth is not limited to *one* local church, *one* denomination, or *one* tradition. We need to be open to truth, and always exercising ourselves to discern good and evil (Heb. 5:14; 1 John 4:1).

Roman Catholicism has instilled fear and suspicion into its adherents. As a result they are afraid to enter a non-Catholic meeting place, or to read "Protestant" books. However, the same kind of fear and suspicion is present in the ranks of non-Catholicism. The fact that the "truth" both sides claim to have must be defended in unChristlike ways should cause us to be watchful and mature in this regard.

This originally appeared in *Searching Together,* 14:1, Spring, 1985.

CHAPTER 27

RE-THINKING "LEADERSHIP" IN THE NEW TESTAMENT

Frank Viola

[The following is an abridged excerpt from Frank Viola's book, Reimagining Church *(David C. Cook, 2008), the Appendix. Used with permission.]*

IS THE NEW TESTAMENT HIERARCHICAL?

For centuries, certain texts in the N.T. have been mishandled to support hierarchical/positional leadership structures in the church. This mishandling has caused no small damage to the body of Christ.

The notion of hierarchical/positional authority is partly the result of mistranslations and misinterpretations of certain biblical passages. These mistranslations and misinterpretations have been influenced by cultural biases that have cluttered the original meaning of the biblical language. Such biases have transformed simple words into heavily loaded ecclesiastical titles. As a result, they have eroded the original landscape of the church. Thus a fresh reading of the N.T. in its original language is necessary for properly understanding certain texts. For instance, a look at the original Greek yields the following insights:

1. "Bishops" are simply guardians *(episkopoi)*, not high-church officials

2. "Pastors" are caretakers *(poimen)*, not professional pulpiteers

3. "Ministers" are table-waiters *(diakonos)*, not clergymen

4. "Elders" are wise old men *(presbuteros)*, not ecclesiastical officers

Thankfully, a growing number of N.T. scholars are pointing out that the "leadership" terminology of the N.T. possesses descriptive accents denoting special functions rather than formal positions. Caring/serving in N.T. is non-official, non-titular, and non-hierarchical.

DOESN'T ACTS 1:20; ROMANS 11:13; 12:4; AND 1 TIMOTHY 3:1, 10, 12 SPEAK OF CHURCH "OFFICIALS"?

The word *office* in these passages is a mistranslation. It has no equivalent in the original Greek. Nowhere in the Greek N.T. do we find the equivalent of *office* used in connection with any ministry, function, or leader in the church.

The Greek word for *office* is only used to refer to the Lord Jesus Christ in His high priestly office (Heb. 5-7). It's also used to refer to the Levitical priesthood (Luke 1:8). The King James Version mistranslates Romans 11:13b to be, "I magnify mine office." But the Greek word translated "office" means service, not office. So a better translation of Romans 11:13b is "I magnify my service *[diakonia]*." Similarly, Romans 12:4b is better translated "All the members do not have the same function *[praxis]*." The Greek word praxis means a doing, a practice, or a function rather than an office or position. The NIV and the NASB reflect this better translation. Finally, 1 Timothy 3:1, says the following in the KJV: "If a man desire the office of a bishop..." But a more accurate translation puts it this way: "If anyone aspires to oversight..."

DOESN'T ACTS 20:28; 1 THESSALONIANS 5:12; 1 TIMOTHY 5:17; AND HEBREWS13:7, 17, 24 SAY THAT ELDERS HAVE "THE RULE OVER" THE CHURCH?

The words "rule" and "over" in these texts are a poor fit with the rest of the New Testament. And there's no analog for them in the Greek text. This is yet another case where certain translations have confused the modern reader by employing culturally conditioned religious terminology.

The word "rule" in Hebrews 13:7, 17, 24 is translated from the Greek word *hegeomai*. It simply means to guide or go before. In his translation of Hebrews, N.T. scholar F. F. Bruce translates *hegeomai* as "guides." This word carries the thought of "those who guide you" rather than "those who rule over you."

Similarly, in 1 Thessalonians 5:12, the word "over" is translated from the Greek word *proistemi*. It carries the idea of standing in front of, superintending, guarding, and providing care for. Robert Banks and F. F. Bruce explain that this term doesn't carry the technical force of an official designation, for it's used in the participle rather than the noun form. It's also positioned as the second in the midst of two other non-official participles. Bruce translates 1 Thessalonians 5:12-13 as follows: "Now we ask you brethren to know those who work hard among you and care for you in the Lord and instruct you, and esteem them very highly in love because of their work."

The same word *(proistemi)* appears in 1 Timothy 5:17. It, too, is incorrectly translated "rule" in the KJV and NASB. In addition, in Acts 20:28, the Greek text says that the elders are *"en"* (among) the flock rather than "over" them (as the KJV puts it). In a similar vein, Paul's statement that overseers must "rule *[proistemi]* their own houses well" in 1 Timothy 3:4-5 doesn't point to their ability to wield power. It rather points to their capacity to supervise, manage, and nurture others. Incidentally, managing the household didn't envision managing the nuclear family. It involved much more than that. It involved managing married and unmarried relatives as well as servants.

In all these passages, the basic thought is that of watching rather than bossing; superintending rather than dominating, facilitating rather than dictating, guiding rather than ruling. The Greek text conveys an image of one who stands within the flock, guarding and caring for it (as a leading-servant would). It's reminiscent of a shepherd who looks out for the sheep—not one who drives them from behind or rules them from above. Again, the thrust of apostolic teaching consistently demonstrates that God's idea of church leadership is at odds with those conventional leadership roles that are based on top-heavy rule.

EVERY PHYSICAL BODY HAS A HEAD. THEREFORE, EVERY LOCAL BODY OF BELIEVERS NEEDS A HEAD. IF IT DOESN'T HAVE ONE, IT WILL BE CHAOTIC. PASTORS ARE THE HEADS OF LOCAL CHURCHES. THEY ARE LITTLE HEADS UNDER CHRIST'S HEADSHIP.

This idea is born out of the imaginations of fallen humans. There is not a shred of biblical support for such an idea. The Bible *never* refers to a human being as a "head" of a church. This title exclusively belongs to Jesus Christ. He is the *only* Head of each local assembly. The church has no head under His own. Therefore, those who claim to be heads of churches supplant the executive headship of Christ.

DOESN'T HEBREWS 13:17 COMMAND US TO OBEY AND SUBMIT TO OUR LEADERS, IMPLYING THAT CHURCH LEADERS POSSESS OFFICIAL AUTHORITY?

Again, a look at the Greek text proves useful here. The word translated "obey" in Hebrews 13:17 is not the garden-variety Greek word *(hupakouo)* that's usually employed in the N.T. for obedience. Rather, it's the word *peitho. Peitho* means to persuade or to win over. Because this word appears in the middle-passive form in Hebrews 13:17, the text ought to be translated "Allow yourselves to be persuaded by your leaders."

This text appears to be an exhortation to give weight to the instruction of local overseers (and possibly apostolic workers). It's not an exhortation to obey them mindlessly. It implies persuasive power to convince and to win over rather than to coerce, force, or browbeat into submission. In the words of Greek scholar W. E. Vine, "The obedience suggested [in Hebrews 13:17] is not by submission to authority, but resulting from persuasion."

Likewise, the verb translated "submit" in this passage is the word *hupeiko*. It carries the idea of yielding, retiring, or withdrawing, as in surrendering after battle. Those who occupy themselves with spiritual oversight don't demand submission. By virtue of their wisdom and spiritual maturity, they are to be accorded with respect.

Christians are encouraged to be uncommonly biased toward what they say. Not because of an external office they hold, but because of their godly character, spiritual stature, and sacrificial service to the people of God. In the words of Hebrews 13:7, we are to "imitate their faith" as we "consider the outcome of their life." By so doing, we make their God-called task of spiritual oversight far easier to carry out (v. 17).

DON'T THE SEVEN ANGELS OF THE SEVEN CHURCHES IN THE BOOK OF REVELATION REPRESENT THE PRESENCE OF A SINGLE PASTOR IN EACH LOCAL CHURCH?

The first three chapters of Revelation constitute a flimsy basis upon which to construct the doctrine of "single pastor." First, the reference to the angels of these churches is cryptic. John doesn't give us any clues about their identity. Scholars are not sure what they symbolize. (Some believe they point to literal angels. Others believe they are human messengers.)

Second, there's no analog for the idea of a "solo pastor" anywhere in the New Testament. Nor is there any text that likens pastors unto angels. Third, the idea that the seven angels refer to the "pastors" of the seven churches is in direct conflict with other N.T. texts. For instance, Acts 20:17 and 20:28 tell us that the church of Ephesus had multiple shepherds (pastors), not one. This is true for all 1st Century churches that had elders. They were always plural.

Therefore, to hang the *"sola pastora"* doctrine on one obscure passage in Revelation is sloppy and careless exegesis. The fact is, there is no support for the modern pastor in Revelation or in any other N.T. document.

THE MESS WE FIND OURSELVES IN TODAY

The primary reason why our ideas on church leadership have strayed so far from God's will can be traced to our tendency to project Western political notions of government onto the biblical writers—reading them back into the text. When we read words like "pastor," "overseer," and "elder," we immediately think in terms of governmental offices like "president," "senator," and "chairman." So we regard elders, pastors, and overseers as sociological constructs (offices). We view them as vacant slots that possess a reality independent of the persons who populate them. We then ascribe mere men with unquestioned authority simply because they "hold office."

The N.T. notion of leadership is markedly different. As previously stated, there's no biblical warrant for the idea that church leadership is official. Neither is there any scriptural backing for the notion that some believers have authority over other believers. The only authority that exists in the church is Jesus Christ. Humans have no authority in themselves. Divine authority is vested only in the Head and expressed through the body. Good leadership, therefore, is never authoritarian. It only displays authority when it's expressing the mind of Jesus Christ.

The basic tasks of biblical leadership are facilitation, nurture, guidance, and service. To the degree that a member is modeling the will of God in one of those areas, to that degree he or she is leading. It's no wonder that Paul never chose to use any of the forty-plus common Greek words for "office" and "authority" when discussing leaders. Again, Paul's favorite word for describing leadership is the opposite of what natural minds would suspect. It's *diakonos,* which means a "servant"—a person very low on the social totem pole in the 1st Century.

FOOD FOR THOUGHT

FURTHER AVENUES FOR READING ABOUT "AUTHORITY"-RELATED MATTERS

Luis F. Acosta, "Hermeneutics & the Development of the Canon," *Ministry,* January, 1998, pp. 24-25, 27

Lord Acton, *Essays On Church & State,* Thomas Y. Crowell Co., 1968, 518 pp.

Lord Acton. "The Protestant Theory of Persecution," *Essays on Freedom & Power, World Publishing,* 1948, 113-141

Theodore W. Adorno, et al., *The Authoritarian Personality,* Abridged Edition, W.W. Norton, 1993, 493 pp.

Roland Allen, *The Ministry of the Spirit,* Eerdmans, 1965, 208 pp.

Gordon W. Allport, *The Nature of Prejudice,* Doubleday-Anchor, 1958, 496 pp.

Randall Arthur, *Wisdom Hunter,* Multnomah Press, 2009, 325 pp.

"Authoritarianism in the Church: The Abuse of Leadership" [articles by Paul Sue, Richard Damiani, Jon Zens] *Searching Together,* Summer-Autumn, 2001, 29:2-3, 37 pp.

Wes Avram, ed., *Anxious About Empire: Theological Essays on the New Global Realities,* Brazos Press, 2004, 215 pp.

Janis & Wesley Balda, "The Four Signs of a Toxic Leader," http://www.qideas.org/blog/the-four-signs-of-a-toxic-leader.aspx

Janis & Wesley Balda, *Handbook for Battered Leaders,* IVP, 2013, 223 pp.

Lee Ann Banaszak, Karen Beckwith, Dieter Rucht, *Women's Movements Facing the Reconfigured State,* Cambridge University Press, 2003, 350 pp.

Robert Banks, *Paul's Idea of Community: The Early House Churches in Their Historical Setting,* Eerdmans, 1980, 208 pp.

William Barclay, *By What Authority?* (Judson, 1975), 221 pages

Paul Barnett, *Is the New Testament Reliable? A Look at the Historical Evidence,* IVP, 1992, 173 pp.

Jerram Barrs, *Shepherds & Sheep: A Biblical View of Leading & Following,* (IVP, 1983), 95 pages

Harold Bauman, *Congregations & Their Servant Leaders: Some Aids for Faithful Congregational Relationships,* Mennonite Publishing House, 1982, 112 pp.

Hendrik Berkof, *Christ & the Powers,* John H. Yoder, translator, Herald Press, 1977, 79 pp.

Pierre Berton, "The Ecclesiastical Caste System," *The Comfortable Pew,* Lippincott, 1965, pp. 61-68

Ernest Best, "Spiritual Sacrifice: General Priesthood in the New Testament," *Interpretation: A Journal of Bible & Theology,* 14:3, July, 1960, pp. 273-299

Harry Bethel, *It's A Man's World: A Fresh Look at a Truth Obscured by the End-Time Apostasy,* 3rd edition, 1996, 18 pp.

Stephen Board, "Is Faith a High-Wire Act," *Eternity,* July/Aug., 1981, 13-16, 26

Stephen B. Bond, *Spiritual Authority: God's Way of Growing Leaders,* College Press, 1995, 172 pp.

Alan Booth, *Christians & Power Politics,* SCM Press, 1963, 127 pp.

Theodore Dwight Bozeman, "Inductive & Deductive in Politics: Science & Society in Antebellum Presbyterian Thought," *The Journal of American History,* 64:3, December, 1977, pp. 704-722

Robert Brinsmead, "Jesus & the Law," *Verdict,* October, 1981, pp. 5-30

Robert Brinsmead, "Religion & Violence," *Verdict,* Essay 35, 1988, pp. 2-13

Robert Brinsmead, "Savage Christians," *Verdict,* Essay 30, 1987, 4 pp.

Robert Brinsmead, "The Gospel & the Spirit of Biblicism – Part 1," Essay 15, *The Christian Verdict*, 1984, pp. 3-9; "The Gospel & the Spirit of Biblicism – Part 2," Essay 16, *The Christian Verdict*, 1984, pp. 2-10

Robert Brinsmead, "The Spirit of Jesus versus Christianity," *Verdict*, 1986, pp. 2-11

Robert Brinsmead, "The Old & the New Law According to the Early Fathers," *Verdict Report*, January, 1983, pp. 1-3

Rita N. Brock & Rebecca A. Parker, *Saving Paradise: How Christianity Traded Love of This World for Crucifixion & Empire*, Beacon Press, 2008, 552 pp.

Lavonn D. Brown, "Who Controls the Bible?" *Baptists Today*, May, 2003, p. 31

F.F. Bruce, *The English Bible: A History of Translations*, Oxford University Press, 1961, 234 pp.

F.F. Bruce, *The Spreading Flame: The Rise & Progress of Christianity*, Eerdmans, 1954, 554 pp.

George Bryson, "Excuse for Abuse: An Examination of Heavy-handed Authority Doctrines," *The Word For Today*, 1990, 7 pages

Gary M. Burge, *The Anointed Community: The Holy Spirit in the Johannine Tradition*, Eerdmans, 1987

Harold L Bussell, *Unholy Devotion: Why Cults Lure Christians* (Zondervan, 1983), 128 pages

Florence Bulle, *God Wants You Rich, and Other Enticing Doctrines*, (Bethany House, 1983)

J. Lawrence Burkholder, "The Concept of the Hermeneutic Community," *Concern* #14, Feb., 1967, p. 72ff

William R. Byers, *The History of the King James Bible & the People Called 'Baptist,'* Sturgis SD, 1987, five cassettes with syllabus

Ted Byfield, General Editor, *The Christians: Their First Two Thousand Years, Christian History Project* – Volume 2, *A Pinch of Incense: A.D. 70 to 250*, 2002, 288 pages; Volume 3, *By This Sign: A.D. 250 to 350*, 2004, 289 pages; Volume 3, *Darkness Descends: A.D. 350 to 565*, 2003, 288 pages; Volume 4, *The Sword of Islam: A.D. 565 to 740*, 2004, 288 pages; Volume 5, *The Quest for the City: A.D. 740 to 1100*, 2004, 288 pages

Daniel Callahan, Heiko Obermann, Daniel O'Hanlon, eds., *Christianity Divided: Protestant & Roman Catholic Theological Issues*, Sheed & Ward, 1964, 335 pp. (articles by Hans Kung, Karl Barth, Oscar Cullmann, T.F. Torrence, E. Schillebeeckx, et al.)

Averil Cameron, "Church and Society," *The Mediterranean World in Late Antiquity, AD 395 – 600*, Routledge, 1993, pp. 57-80

Campaginator, *Priesthood & Clergy Unknown to Christianity; or, The Church A Community of Co-Equal Brethren,* Philadelphia: J. B. Lippincott & Co., 1857, 145 pp.

Anthony Campolo, Jr., *The Power Delusion: A Serious Call to Consider Jesus' Approach to Power,* Victor Books, 1989, 165 pp.

Peter M. Candler, Jr., T*heology, Rhetoric, Manuduction, or Reading Scripture Together on the Path to God,* SCM Press, 2006, 190 pp.

D.A. Carson, editor, *Worship by the Book,* Zondervan, 2002, 256 pp.

Shirley Jackson Case, *The Evolution of Early Christianity,* University of Chicago Press, 1942, 385 pp.

Nancy L. Clark & William Worger, *South Africa: The Rise & Fall of Apartheid,* Pearson/ Longman, 2004, 173 pp.

Steve Coleman. "A Christian Look at the Shepherding Movement," *Personal Freedom Outreach,* 3:2.

Robert & Mary Coote, *Power, Politics, & the Making of the Bible: An Introduction,* Fortress, 1990, 291 pp.

Carl P. Cosaert, "The Reliability of the New Testament Scriptures: Earliest Manuscript Evidence," Part 1, *Ministry,* September, 2011, pp. 6-9; "The Reliability of the New Testament Scriptures: Early Christians & the Codex," Part 2, *Ministry,* November, 2011, pp. 21-24

Richard H. Cox, *Rewiring Your Preaching: How the Brain Processes Sermons,* IVP, 2012, 182 pp.

Leon Cristiani, *Heresies & Heretics,* Hawthorn Books, 1959, 142 pp.

Michael H. Crosby, *The Dysfunctional Church: Addiction & Co-Dependency in the Family of Catholicism,* Ave Maria Press, 1991, 256 pp.

Albert J. Dager, *Vengeance Is Ours: The Church in Dominion,* Sword Publishers, 1990, 283 pp.

Amaury de Riencourt, *The Coming Caesars,* Omaha, NE, Trestle Press, 2013, formerly: New York: Coward-McCann, 1957

Leo Donald Davis, *The First Seven Ecumenical Councils (325 - 787): Their History & Theology,* The Liturgical Press, 1990, 342 pp.

Sara Diamond, *Spiritual Warfare: The Politics of the Christian Right, South End Press,* 1989, 292 pp.

Thomas Dubay, "Communication in Community," *Searching Together,* Winter, 1985, pp. 1-14

Dean Dudley, *History of the First Council of Nice with A Life of Constantine*, A & B Publishers Group, 1992, 110 pp.

Avery Dulles, "Revelation as the Basis for Scripture & Tradition," *Evangelical Review of Theology*, 21:2, 1997, pp. 104-120; "Scripture & Tradition: An Evangelical Response," Henri Blocher, *ERT*, 21:2, 1997, pp. 121-127

David L. Dungan, *Constantine's Bible: Politics & the Making of the New Testament*, SCM Press, 2006, 224 pp.

Umberto Eco, "The Force of Falsity," *Serendipities: Language & Lunacy*, Harcourt-Brace, 1999, pp. 1-21

Bart D. Ehrman, "The Rise of Early Christian Orthodoxy," *Lost Christianities: Christian Scriptures and the Battles Over Authentication*, The Great Courses, 2002, pp. 286-302

Helen Ellerbe, *The Dark Side of Christian History*, Morningstar & Lark, 5th printing, 1999, 219 pp.

Werner Elert, *Eucharist & Church Fellowship in the First Four Centuries*, Concordia, 1966, 231 pp.

Charles Elliott, *Comfortable Compassion? Poverty, Power & the Church*, Paulist Press, 1987, 194 pp.

Ronald M. Enroth, "The Power Abusers: When follow-the-leader becomes a dangerous game," *Eternity*, Oct., 1979, 23-27

Philip F. Esler, ed., *Modelling Early Christianity: Social-Scientific Studies of the New Testament in Its Context*, Routledge, 2004, 349 pp.

David Estrada & William White, Jr., *The First New Testament*, Thomas Nelson, 1978, 144 pp.

Heinz Eulau, *The Behavioral Persuasion in Politics*, Random House, 1966, 141p pp.

Alexandre Faivre, *The Emergence of the Laity in the Early Church*, Paulist Press, 1990, 242 pp.

Steven Fanning, *Mystics of the Christian Tradition*, Routledge, 2001, 279 pp.

Gordon D. Fee, "Praying & Prophesying in the Assemblies: 1 Cor. 11:2-16," *Discovering Biblical Equality*, Pierce/Grootuis editors, IVP, 2004, pp. 142-160

Cheryl Forbes, *The Religion of Power*, Zondervan, 1983, 144 pp.

George W. Forell, *History of Christian Ethics, Volume 1, From the New Testament to Augustine*, Augsburg Publishing House, 1979, 247 pp.

Ruth Irene Garrett, *Crossing Over: One Woman's Escape from Amish Life,* Harper, 2003, 190 pp.

Winfred E. Garrison, *Intolerance,* Round Table Press, 1934, 270 pp.

Keith Giles, *The Power of Weakness,* 2012, 97 pp.

Kevin Giles, *Patterns of Ministry Among the First Christians,* CollinsDove, 1992, 247 pp.

Donald J. Goergen, *The Jesus of Christian History,* The Liturgical Press, 1992, 287 pp.

Justo L. Gonzalez, *The Story of Christianity: The Reformation to the Present Day, Volume 2,* Harper, 1985, 414 pp.

Edgar J. Goodspeed, *How Came the Bible?,* Abingdon, 1940, 148 pp.

Edgar J. Goodspeed, *The Formation of the New Testament,* University of Chicago Press, 1974, 210 pp.

Henry G. Graham, *Where We Got the Bible: Our Debt to the Catholic Church,* Tan Books & Publishers, 17th printing, 1977, 154 pp.

Robert M. Grant, *The Formation of the New Testament,* Hutchinson University Library, 1965, 195 pp.

Rodney A. Gray, "Love One Another: Crucial Implications for Healthy Church Life," *Searching Together,* 16:3, 1987, 16 pp.

J. Harold Greenlee, *Scribes, Scrolls & Scripture,* Eerdmans, 1985, 102 pp.

Stanley J. Grenz, *Revisioning Evangelical Theology: A Fresh Agenda for the 21st Century,* IVP, 1993, 208 pp.

Rosine Hammett & Loughlan Sofield, *Inside Christian Community,* Le Jacq Publishing, 1981, 146 pp.

Gabriel Hebert, *Fundamentalism & the Church,* Westminster Press, 1957, 156 pp.

William G. Heidt, *Old-New Testament Reading Guide: Inspiration, Canonicity, Tests, Versions, Hermeneutics – A General Guide to Sacred Scripture,* The Liturgical Press, 1970, 123 pp.

Christopher Hill, *The English Bible & the 17th Century Revolution,* Penguin Books, 1994, 466 pp.

Russell T. Hitt, "The Soul Watchers," *Eternity,* April 1976, 13-15, 34, 36-37

Dee Hock, *Leadership: One From Many,* PDF

Charles Holt, "Questions for the Editor (No. 2)," *The Examiner,* 5:3, May, 1990, pp. 2-3

H. Wayne House, *The Role of Women in Ministry Today,* Thomas Nelson, 1990, 192 pp.

William Howitt, *A Popular History of Priestcraft in All Ages & Nations* [1833], Milton Printing, 1982, 304 pp.

Roger Huber, *No Middle Ground: A Celebration of the Liberation from Religion,* Abingdon Press, 1971, 155 pp.

Arland J. Hultgren & Steven A. Haggmark, *The Earliest Christian Heretics: Readings from Their Opponents,* Fortress Press, 1996, 199 pp.

Werner Jaeger, *Early Christianity & Greek Paideia,* Belknap Press, 1965, 154 pp.

Daniel Jenkins, *Tradition & the Spirit,* Faber & Faber, 1951, 195 pp.

Philip Jenkins, *Jesus Wars: How Four Patriarchs, Three Queens, and Two Emperors Decided What Christians Would Believe for the Next 1,500 Years,* HarperOne, 2010, 328 pp.

David Johnson & Jeff VanVonderen, *The Subtle Power of Spiritual Abuse,* Bethany House, 1991, 234 pp.

Laurie Beth Jones, *Jesus, CEO: Using Ancient Wisdom for Visionary Leadership,* Hyperion, 1994, 309 pp.

Tony Jones, *The Church Is Flat: The Relational Ecclesiology of the Emerging Church Movement,* The JoPa Group, 2011, 212 pp.

John Kater, Jr., "God & Power," *Christians on the Right: The Moral Majority in Perspective,* Seabury, 1982, p. 38ff.

Paul Kenley, "Reconciling Pastoral Leadership & the Priesthood of the Believer," *Baptists Today,* July, 2000, p. 25

George A. Kennedy, *Classical Rhetoric & Its Christian and Secular Tradition from Ancient to Modern Times, 2nd Edition,* University of North Carolina Press, 1999, 345 pp.

Robert C. Kiste, *The Bikinians: A Study in Forced Migration,* Cummings Publishing Co., 1974, 212 pp.

Meredith Kline, *Images of the Spirit,* Baker, 1980, 142 pp.

Meredith G. Kline, *The Structure of Biblical Authority, 2nd Edition,* Eerdmans, 1975, 218 pp.

Adriene Koch, *Power, Morals & the Founding Fathers: Essays in the Interpretation of the American Enlightenment,* Cornell University Press, 1975, 158 pp.

Andreas J. Kostenberger & David Croteau, eds., *Which Bible Translation Should I Use?*, B & H Publishing Group, 2012, 204 pp.

Hans Kung, *The Catholic Church: A Short History*, The Modern Library, 2003, 230 pp.

Hans Kung, *Why Priests? A Proposal for a New Church Ministry*, Doubleday, 1972, 118 pp.

John Laux, Church History: A Complete History of the Catholic Church to the Present Day [1945], Tan Books & Publishers, 1989, vol. 2, pp. 297-663

Leadership and Authority in the Church, Mennonite Pub. House, 1979, 60 pages.

Alan Lear, "Concerns About Traditional Ministry Patterns: An African Perspective," *Searching Together*, 24:4, 1996, pp. 1-14

Philip J. Lee, *Against the Protestant Gnostics*, Oxford University Press, 1987, 347 pp.

Paul Lehmann, *Ethics in a Christian Context*, Harper & Row, 1963, 384 pp.

Alfred Liosy, *The Origins of the New Testament*, George Allen & Unwin Ltd., 1950, 332 pp.

Franklin H. Littell, *The Church & the Body Politic*, Seabury Press, 1969, 175 pp.

D.M. Lloyd-Jones, *Authority: of Jesus Christ, of the Scriptures, of the Holy Spirit*, Banner of Truth, 1992, 94 pp.

Eduard Lohse, *The Formation of the New Testament*, Abingdon, 1981, 256 pp.

H. B. London, Jr., ed., "What I Like About Being A Pastor," *Focus on the Family: Pastor to Pastor*, 2003, 2 CD's

Richard Longenecker, *The Ministry & Message of Paul*, Zondervan, 1980.

Ernest G. Loosley, *When the Church Was Very Young*, George Allen & Unwin, 1935, 119 pp.

Pat MacMillan, *The Performance Factor: Unlocking the Secrets of Teamwork*, Broadman/Holman, 2001, 336 pp.

George Martin, ed., *Scripture & the Charismatic Movement: Proceedings of the Milwaukee Symposium*, December 1-3, 1978, Servant Books, 1979, 127 pp.

Mark M. Mattison, "The Rise of the Clergy," Unpublished paper, ca. 1991, 8 pp.

Willi Marxsen, *The New Testament as the Church's Book*, Fortress Press, 1976, 154 pp.

C.C. McCown, *Codex & Roll in the New Testament*, reprinted from The Harvard Theological Review, 34:4, October, 1941, pp. 219-250

Matthew & Christa McKirland, *"Who's In Charge? Questioning Our Common Assumptions about Spiritual Authority,"* Priscilla Papers, 27:1, 2013, pp. 15-25

J. Jeffrey Means (with contributions by Mary Ann Nelson), "Three Dilemmas Facing the Church," *Trauma & Evil: Healing the Wounded Soul,* Fortress Press, 2000, pp. 178-182

Bruce M. Metzger, *The New Testament: Its Background, Growth, and Content,* Abingdon, 1965, 288 pp.

Donald Meyer, *The Positive Thinkers: A Study of the American Quest for Health, Wealth & Personal Power from Mary Baker Eddy to Norman Vincent Peale,* Anchor-Doubleday, 1966, 342 pp.

Alvera Mickelsen, ed., *Women, Authority & the Bible,* IVP, 1986, 304 pp.

Maria Mies, *Patriarchy & Accumulation on a World Scale: Women in the International Division of Labour,* Zed Books, 1998, 251 pp.

Stanley Milgram, *Obedience to Authority: An Experimental View,* Perennial, 2004, 224 pp.

Alice Miller, "Gurus and Cult Leaders: How They Function," *Paths of Life, Seven Scenarios,* Vintage Books, 1999, pp. 141-149

Hal Miller, "The Pastor's Authority," *Ekklesia: To the Roots of Biblical Church Life,* NTRF, February, 2003, pp. 63-67.

C. Wright Mills, *The Power Elite,* Oxford University Press, 1972, 423 pp.

Dafydd Morris, "Christ & the Scriptures," *Quarterly Record,* Trinitarian Bible Society, #602, 2013, pp. 25-28

Stephen Mott, "Intentional Community As A Gift of the Spirit – The Ordering by the Spirit," *Creating An Intentional Community,* John Biersdorf, ed., Abingdon, 1976, pp. 220-233

C.F.D. Moule, *The Birth of the New Testament,* Harper & Row, 1962, 252 pp.

Nicos P. Mouzelis, *Organization & Bureaucracy: An Analysis of Modern Theories,* Aldine Publishing Co., 9th printing, 1976, 230 pp.

Jeremy Myers, "Creeds Kill," www.tillhecomes.org/creeds-kill/

Jeremy Myers, "The Creeds of Christendom," www.tillhecomes.org/the-creeds-of-christendom

Jack Nelson-Pallmeyer, *Jesus Against Christianity: Reclaiming the Missing Jesus,* Trinity Press International, 2001, 368 pp.

D.E. Nineham, ed., *The Church's Use of the Bible: Past & Present,* SPCK, 1963, 174 pp.

Robert Nisbet, *Twilight of Authority*, Oxford University Press, 1977, 287 pp.

Albert Nolan, *Jesus Before Christianity*, Orbis Books, 1978, 156 pp.

Mark A. Noll, "Realities of Empire: The Council of Nicea (325)," *Turning Points: Decisive Moments in the History of Christianity*, 2nd edition, Baker Academic, 2000, pp. 47-64

Henri Nouwen, *In the Name of Jesus: Reflections on Christian Leadership*, The Crossroad Publishing Co., 2002, 107 pp.

Anders Nygren, *The Significance of the Bible for the Church*, Fortress, 1963, 45 pp.

Joan O'Grady, *Early Christian Heresies*, Barnes & Noble, 1994, 157 pp.

Carolyn Osiek & David L. Balch, *Families in the New Testament World: Households & House Churches*, Westminster/John Knox, 1997, 329 pp.

Will Oursler, *Protestant Power & the Coming Revolution: A Frontline Report*, Doubleday & Co., 1971, 203 pp.

Virginia Stem Owens, *The Total Image or Selling Jesus in the Modern Age*, Eerdmans, 1980, 97 pp.

Elaine Pagels, "One God, One Bishop: The Politics of Monotheism," *The Gnostic Gospels*, Vintage books, 1989, 182 pp.

Yvonne Partyka & Joanne Klinger, *Surviving Shattered Dreams: The Story of Two Pastor's Wives*, Wine Press Publishing, 2009, 135 pp.

Constance F. Parvey, "The Theology and Leadership of Women in the New Testament," *Religion & Sexism: Images of Women in the Jewish & Christian Traditions*, R.R. Ruether, ed., Simon & Schuster, 1974, pp. 117-149

Eric Pement, "Built On a Lie: Life in the Children of God," *Cornerstone* Vol.11, #63, 4-6, 8

Ruby Potter, "From Man's Covering to God as Our Covering," *The Church in Transformation*, EkkleFusion, 2012, pp. 160-177

George T. Purves, "The Influence of Paganism on Post-Apostolic Christianity," *The Presbyterian Review*, Vol. 9, #36, 1888, pp. 529-553

Richard Quebedeaux, *By What Authority: The Rise of Personality Cults in American Christianity* (Harper & Row, 1982), 204 pp.

John Reisinger, "A Word About Creeds," *Sound of Grace*, March, 2011, pp. 1-2, 4, 12, 16-17

Johann G. *Rempel, Katechismus in der Wehrlosigkeit: eine kurze biblische Unterweisung in der christlichen Wehrlosigkeit in Frage und Antwort für die Jugend, Rosthern,* Saskatchewan: Druck von D.H. Epp, [194-?], 19 pp.

Rosemary Radford Reuther, "Misogynism & Virginal Feminism in the Father of the Church," *Religion & Sexism,* R.R. Ruether, ed., Simon & Schuster, 1974, pp. 150-183

Larry Richards (Clyde Hoeldtke), *A Theology of Church Leadership,* Zondervan, 1980, 425 pp.

Larry Richards (Gib Martin), *A Theology of Personal Ministry: Spiritual Giftedness in the Local Church,* Zondervan, 1981, 332 pp.

Stephen P. Robbins, *Essentials of Organizational Behavior,* 6th edition, Prentice Hall, 2000, 303 pp.

E.H. Robertson, *The Bible in the Local Church,* Association Press, 1963, 107 pp.

Caleb Rosado, "Lessons from Waco," *Ministry,* July, 1993, pp. 6-11

Ron Rosenbaum, "First Blood: Interview of Bernard Bailyn," *Smithsonian,* March, 2003, pp. 27-34

Anne Rowthorn, *The Liberation of the Laity,* Morehouse Publishing, 1990, 141 pp.

Dale Rumble, *The Diakonate Servant-Leaders,* Destiny Image, 1993, 229 pp.

Auguste Sabatier, *Religions of Authority and the Religion of the Spirit,* McClure, Phillips & Co., 1904, 410 pp.

Graeme Salaman, ed., *Control & Ideology in Organizations,* MIT Press, 1983.

Edward Schillebeeckx and Johann-Baptist Metz, eds., *Concilium: The Right of the Community to a Priest,* March, 1980, 133 pp.

H. Carl Shank, "The Hermeneutics of Anabaptist Thought," *Baptist Reformation Review* (now *Searching Together*), 7:3, 1978, pp. 39-51

Jeff Sharlet, *The Family: The Secret Fundamentalism At the Heart of American Power,* Harper Perennial, 2009, 454 pp.

Lorna A. Shoemaker, "Because There Were So Many of Them! Minority Status in the Middle Ages," *Encounter,* 72:1, 2011, pp. 103-112

Marguerite Shuster, *Power, Pathology, Paradox: The Dynamics of Evil & Good,* Zondervan, 1987, 276 pp.

James W. Sire, *Scripture Twisting: 20 Ways Cults Misread the Bible,* IVP, 1980, 177 pages.

James D. Smart, *The Strange Silence of the Bible in the Church: A Study in Hermeneutics,* Westminster Press, 1970, 186 pp.

Charles Merrill Smith, *The Pearly Gates Syndicate or How to Sell Real Estate in Heaven,* Doubleday, 1971, 220 pp.

Christian Smith, "Do Church Without Clergy," *Going to the Root: Nine Proposals for Radical Church Renewal,* Herald Press, 1992, pp. 36-57.

Christian Smith, *The Bible Made Impossible: Why Biblicism Is Not a Truly Evangelical Reading of Scripture,* Brazos Press, 2011, 220 pp.

James H. Smylie, "Presbyterian Clergy & Problems of 'Dominion' in the Revolutionary Generation," *Journal of Presbyterian History,* 48:3, 1970, pp. 161-175

Lewis W. Spitz, *The Renaissance & Reformation Movements,* Vol. 2, The Reformation, Revised Edition, Concordia Publishing House, 1987, 614 pp.

H.F. Stander & Johannes P. Louw, *Baptism in the Early Church,* Reformation Today Trust, 2004, 192 pp.

Elliot L. Stevens, ed., *Rabbinic Authority: Papers Presented Before the 91st Annual Convention of the Central Conference of American Rabbis,* Vol. XC, Part 2, Central Conference of American Rabbis, 1982, 118 pp.

Peter Stuhlmacher, *Historical Criticism & Theological Interpretation of Scripture,* Fortress, 1977, 93 pp.

R. B. Thieme, Jr. *Canonicity,* 1973, 72 pp.

Charles Tilly, *Coercion, Capital, and European States, AD 990-1992,* Blackwell, 1993, 271 pp.

Hans Toch, *The Social Psychology of Social Movements,* The Bobbs-Merrill Co., 1965, 257 pp.

Peter Toon, *The Right of Private Judgment: The Study & Interpretation of Scripture in Today's Church,* Western Conservative Baptist Seminary, 1976, 23 pp.

Richard Valantasis, *Gnosticism & Other Vanished Christianities,* Three Leaves Press, 2006, 159 pp.

Frank Viola, *Finding Organic Church: A Comprehensive Guide to Starting & Sustaining Authentic Christian Community,* David C. Cook, 2009, 320 pp.

Frank Viola & George Barna, *Pagan Christianity: Exploring the Roots of Our Church Practices,* Tyndale, 2008, 291 pp.

Frank Viola, *Reimagining Church: Pursuing the Dream of Organic Christianity,* David C. Cook, 2008, 318 pp.

Hans Von Campenhausen, E*cclesiastical Authority & Spiritual Power in the Church of the First Three Centuries,* Stanford University Press, 1969, 308 pp.

Rachel C. Wahlberg, *Jesus According to A Woman,* Paulist Press, 1986, 100 pp.

B.F. Westcott, *A General Survey of the History of the Canon of the New Testament,* Macmillan & Co., 1889, 593 pp.

Henry Wiencek, "Master of Monticello: A New Portrait of Thomas Jefferson," *Smithsonian,* October, 2012, pp. 40-49, 92-97.

James R. White, "What Really Happened at Nicea?" *Christian Research Journal,* Spring, 1997, 10 pp.

J.L. Williams, *Victor Paul Wierwille & The Way International,* Moody Press, 1979, 158 pp.

R.R. Williams, *Authority in the Apostolic Age, with Two Essays of the Modern Problem of Authority,* SCM Press, 1950, 144 pp.

Russell Willingham, *Relational Masks: Removing the Barriers that Keep Us Apart,* IVP, 2004, 191 pp.

Garry Wills, *Papal Sin: Structures of Deceit,* Image Books, 2001, 320 pp.

P.B. Wilson, *Liberated Through Submission,* Harvest House Publishers, 1990

Lawrence Wright, "Orphans of Jonestown," *The New Yorker,* November 22, 1993, pp. 66-87

N.T. Wright, "How Can the Bible Be Authoritative?" The Laing Lecture of 1989, *Vox Evangelica,* Vol. 21, 1991, pp. 7-32

Nigel Goring Wright, *Disavowing Constantine: Mission, Church & the Social Order in the Theologies of John Howard Yoder & Jurgen Moltmann,* Paternoster, 2000, 251 pp.

John Yoder, "Binding and Loosing," *Concern* #14, Feb. 1967, 2-31

Jon Zens, "A Review Article of God's Righteous Kingdom – The Law's Connection to the Gospel [by Walter J. Chantry], *Baptist Reformation Review,* 10:1, 1981, pp. 19-31

Jon Zens, "Desiring Unity…Finding Division: Lessons from the 19th Century Restoration Movement," *Searching Together,* 15:3-4, 1986, 33 pp.

ACKNOWLEDGMENTS

This publishing project was realized only because of help from many people. I want to thank all of the contributing authors for their hard work in expressing Kingdom perspectives. Graham Wood spent untold hours taking articles from the past that were never in digital format; turning them into documents I could work with. Many thanks to Rafael Polendo for his labor of love in preparing the cover and formatting the internal text. My heartfelt thanks extend to Greta Bemisderfer, Kat Huff, Bonnie Jaeckle, Arlan Purdy, Leah McConnell Randall, Marv and Jodi Root for their proofreading and helpful suggestions.

The inclusion of numerous authors in this book in no way implies, of course, that any or all of them are in full agreement with the content I have written.

—JZ